ADVERTISING THE BEATLES

A unique look at how Beatles products were merchandised to the world

Photo by Robert Freeman

ADVERTISING THE BEATLES

A unique look at how Beatles products were merchandised to the world

Written and compiled by

Ray Zirkle

HenschelHAUS
Milwaukee, Wisconsin

Copyright © 2018 by Ray Zirkle
All rights reserved.

Advertisements shown in this book are public domain. Images used throughout are from actual advertisements and promotional releases published by Capitol/EMI Records, Apple Records, *Billboard* magazine, and *Cashbox* Magazine.

Published by HenschelHAUS Publishing, Inc.
www.henschelHAUSbooks.com
Milwaukee, Wisconsin, USA

ISBN: 978159598-646-7 (softcover)
ISBN: 978159598-647-4 (hardcover)
E-ISBN: 978159598-649-8 (e-book)

Dedicated to all Beatles fans around the world,
and especially to Paul, George, John, and Ringo

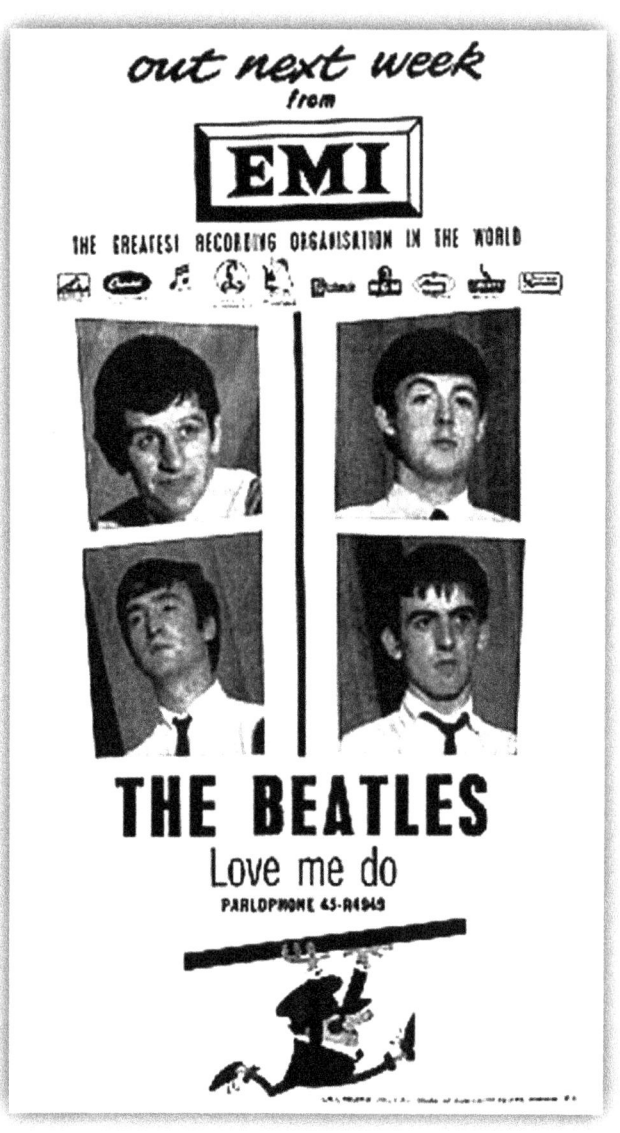

The first two British ads featuring a new, unheard-of group from northern England: The Beatles!

PREFACE

You hold in your hands a visual history of how the most famous band in the world introduced their products to the record-buying public.

I have been a Beatles fan for the past fifty years, with distinct memories of listening to scratchy 45s with their familiar yellow and orange Capitol Records swirl. I played these on a small, portable record player, while my sisters listened to albums like Rubber Soul on our family console. My mother tried to like the music that everyone else loved in the mid-1960s—I don't think she ever succeeded.

I purchased my first Beatles 45 in 1970, just as the group was breaking up. A year later, I bought my first Beatles LP—*Magical Mystery Tour*! I'll never forget thumbing through the pages of the book inside and listening to those songs. My quest for more Beatles music had begun.

On the little bit of money I made delivering newspapers, I started to buy as many records as I could. Of course, my Christmas and birthday wish lists after that included only vinyl.

Beatles memorabilia soon followed. My collection has grown quite a bit over the years. In 2016, I became obsessed with the advertisements used to promote the LPs and started collecting the actual ads. My goal was to put together a visual collection without all the technicalities. Then I thought maybe other Beatles fans would enjoy seeing these one-of-a-kind advertisements, all gathered in one place.

Enjoy this "magical mystery tour"!

~ Ray Zirkle

Advertising the Beatles

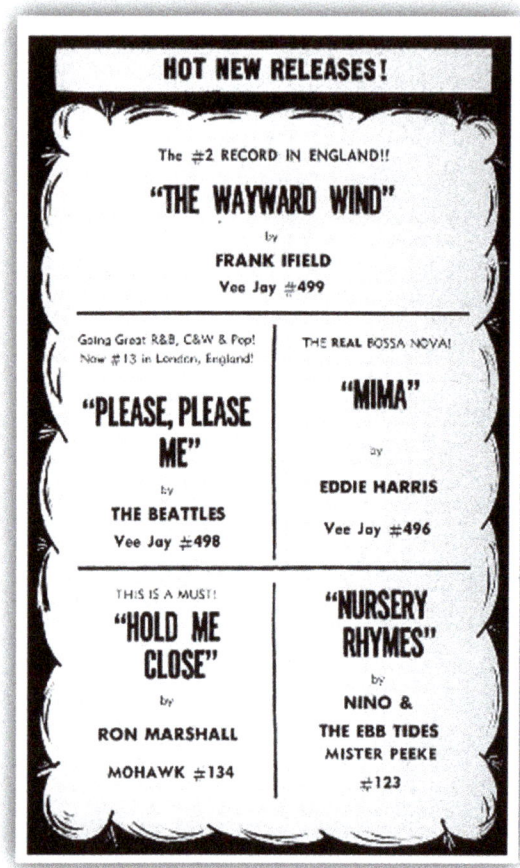

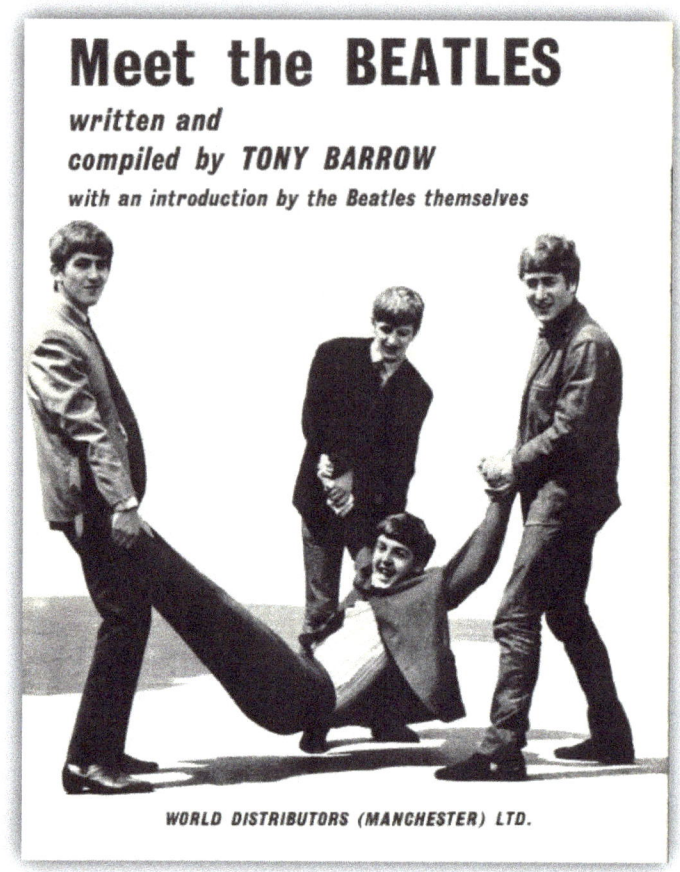

Upper left: VeeJay Record's first ad for *Please, Please Me*.

Upper right: A British promotional flyer introducing the group to record buyers.

Left: The first picture sleeve issued in America for the single, *Please, Please Me*.

ADVERTISING THE BEATLES

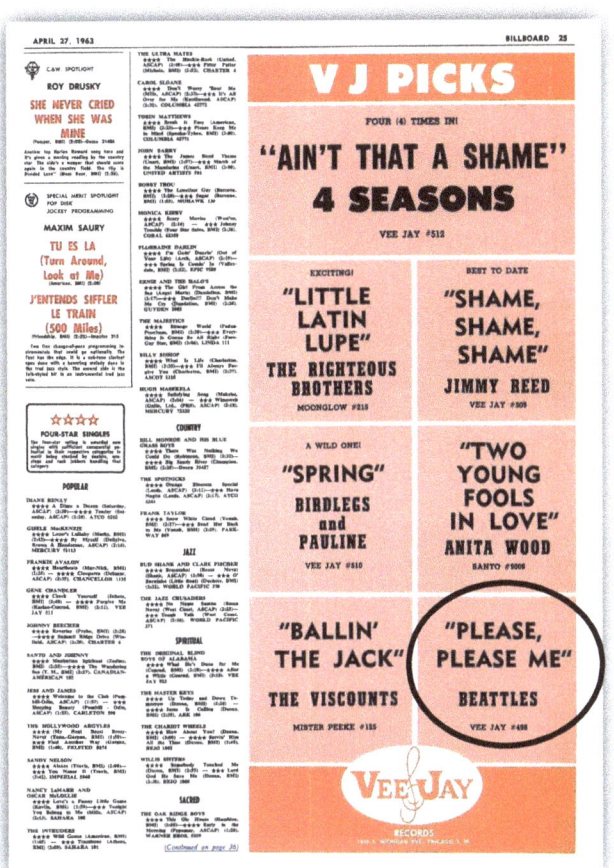

The first couple of American ads featuring the name "Beatles." Of course, the first time it was used, it was spelled wrong (Beattles). Soon the world would know the Beatles name, never to be forgotten.

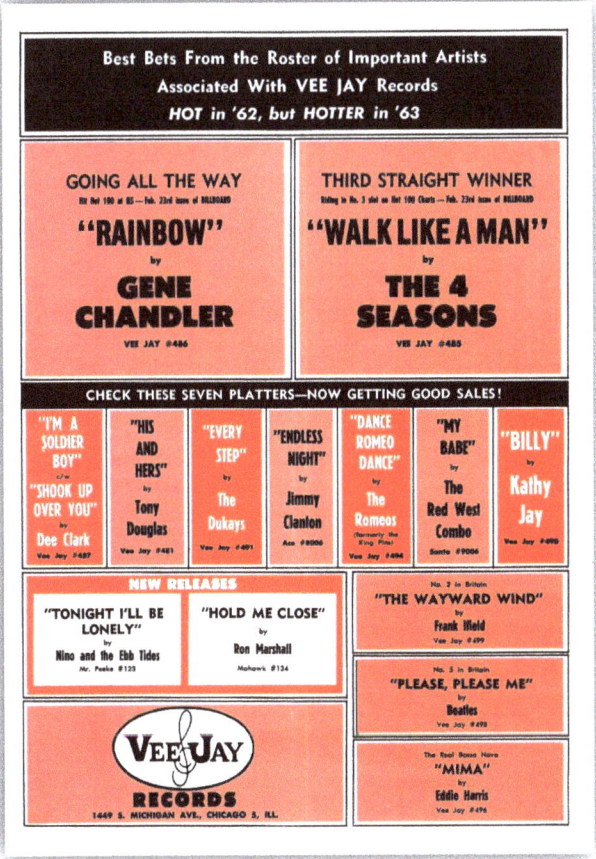

VeeJay Records ads for *Please, Please Me* and *From Me to You*, April 1963.

ADVERTISING THE BEATLES

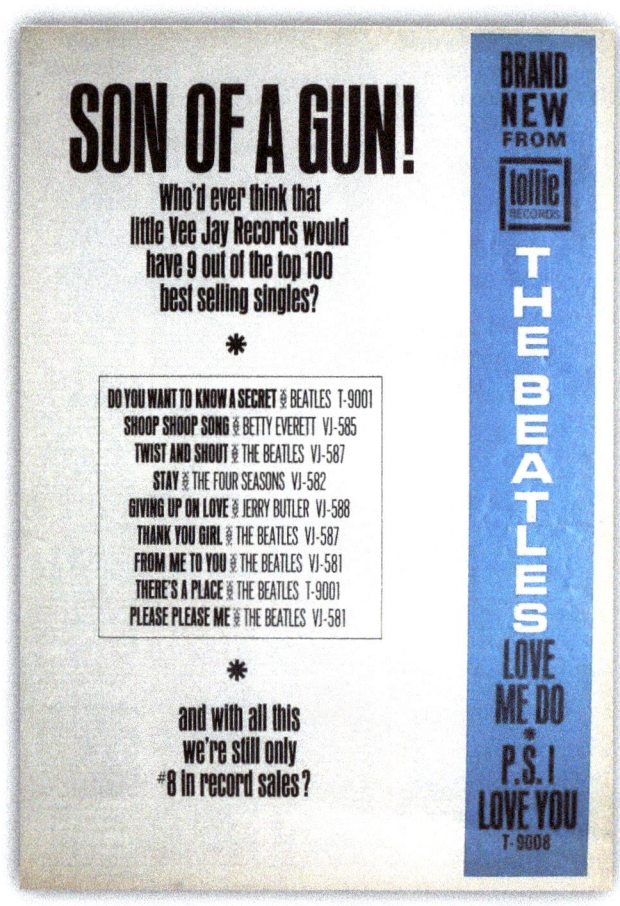

Love Me Do on Tollie Records

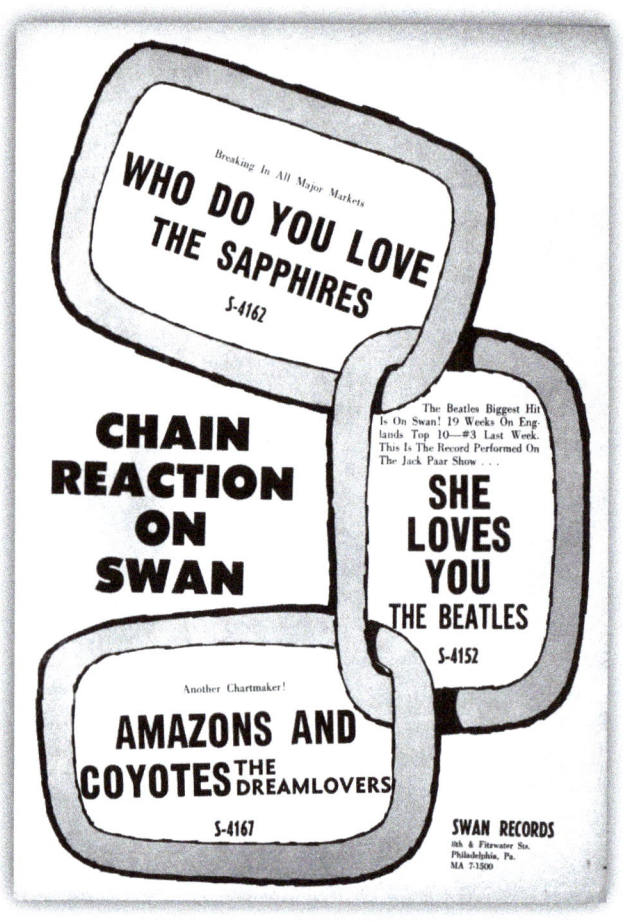

She Loves You on Swan Records

In 1963, Capitol Records had first-refusal rights on any singles or LPs that were routinely offered up by the parent company, EMI. The Beatles were just one of those "pop groups" Capitol decided to pass on. The Beatles' many 45 releases were shopped around to smaller record labels. These had some moderate success with songs that would in time become classics!

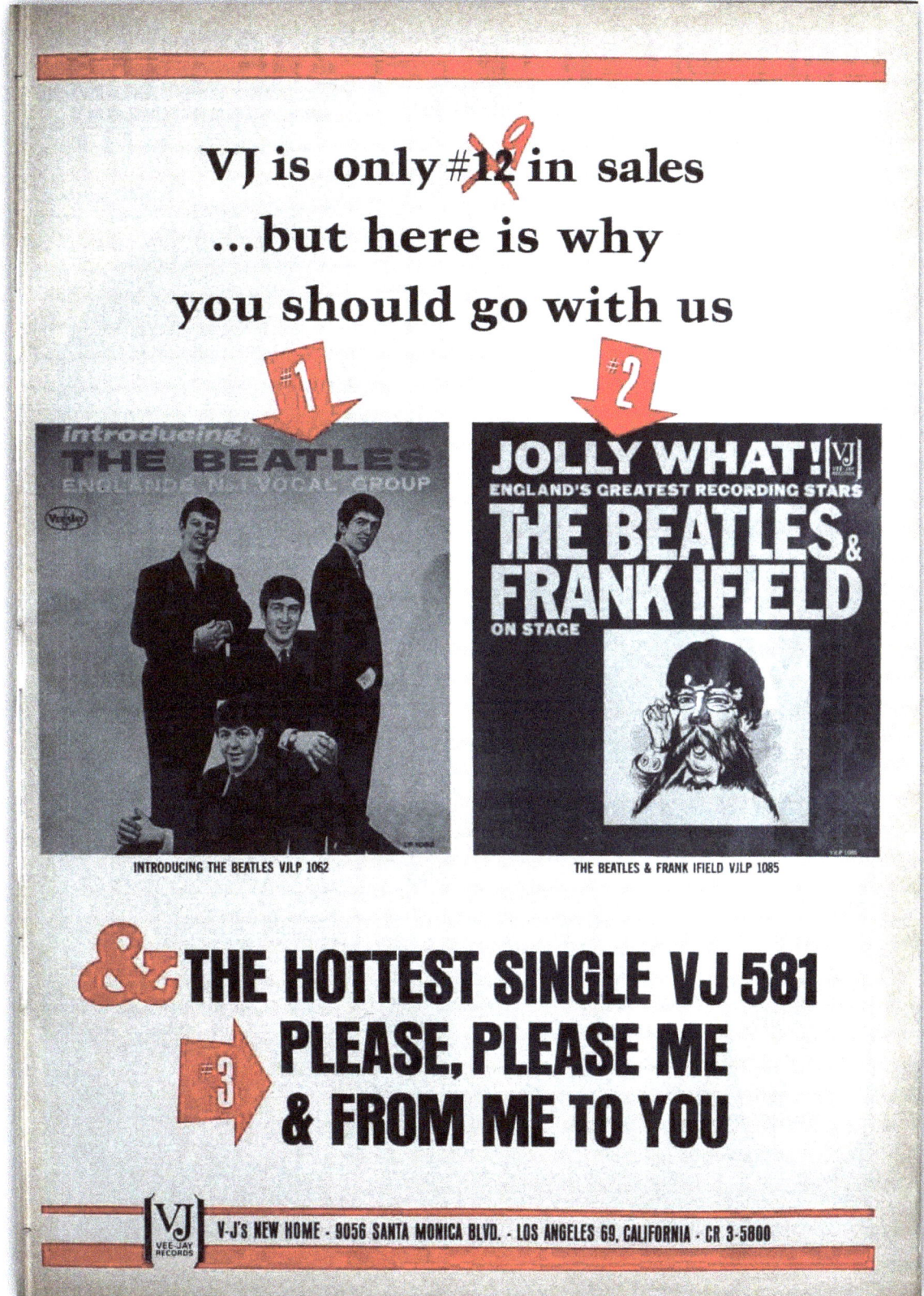

VJ Records of Chicago finally heard the buzz coming from England and acquired the rights to the British *Please, Please Me* LP.

VJ found that it could keep repackaging the same batch of songs, with different covers, even as Capitol began proceedings to stop distribution of the Beatles' songs. Capitol finally realized it was missing the boat on Beatlemania.

This tiny ad in the corner of a January 1964 *Billboard* magazine was enough to spark the interest of record retailers nationwide.

The Beatles' second LP was finished and Capitol Records was ready to listen. Capitol sued the various smaller labels and became the new "Beatles Headquarters."

The ride was about to begin!

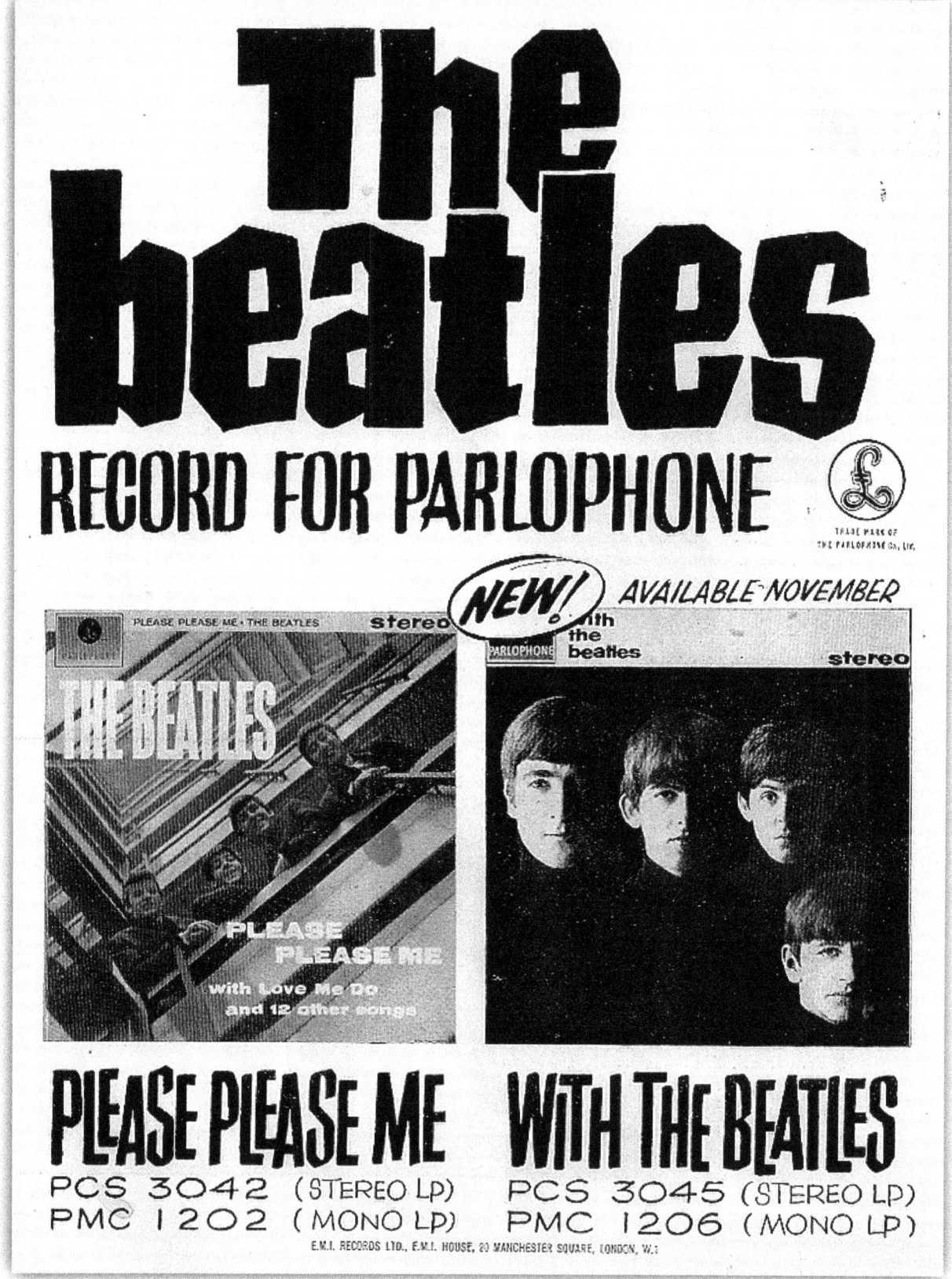

British ads for the Please, Please Me and the With the Beatles LPs on Parlophone.

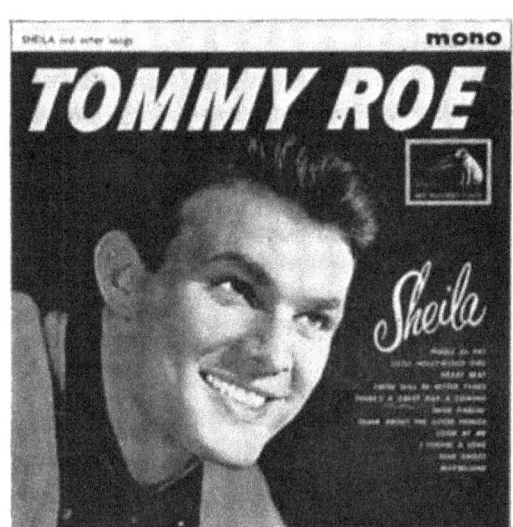

Advertising the Beatles

This image, shot by photographer Dezo Hoffman, was used repeatedly in 1963 and '64. It would become the "look" of the Beatles as they took over the music world.

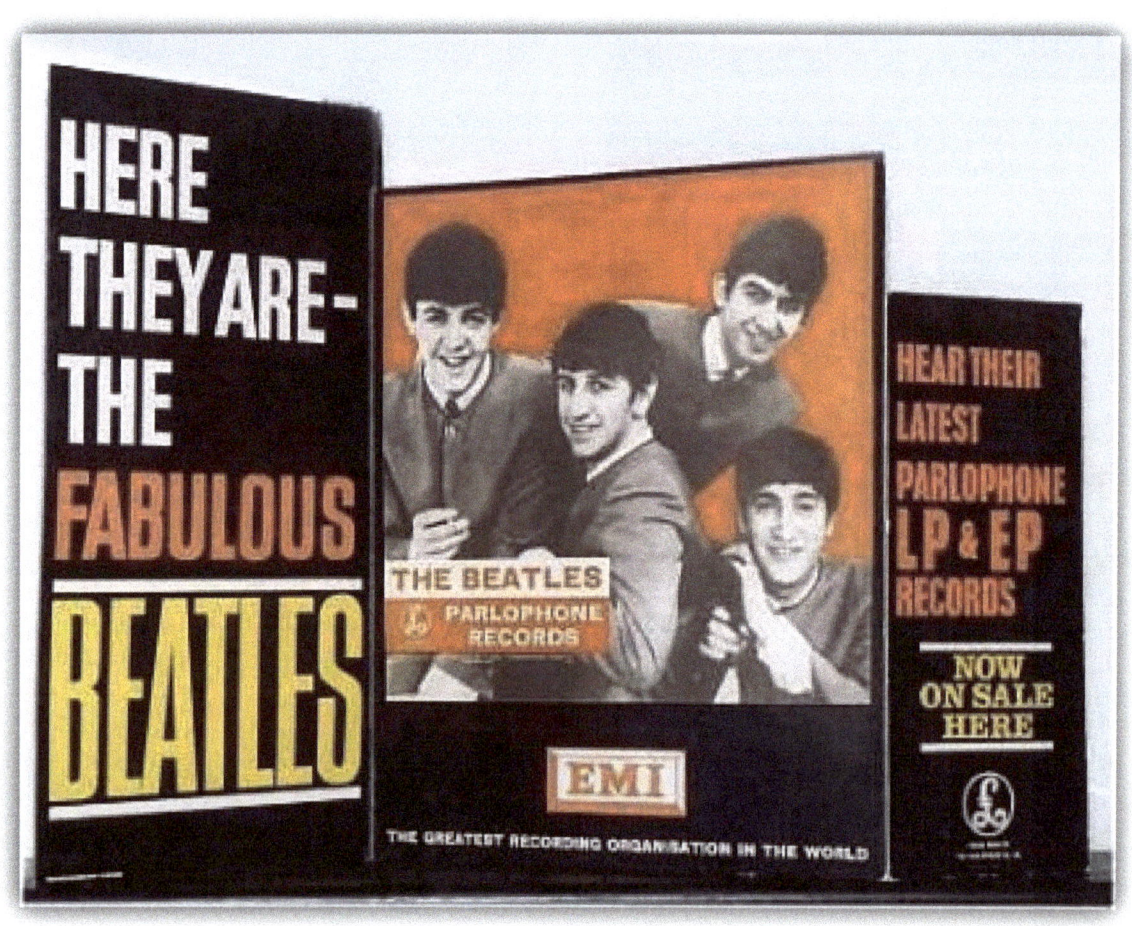

ADVERTISING THE Beatles

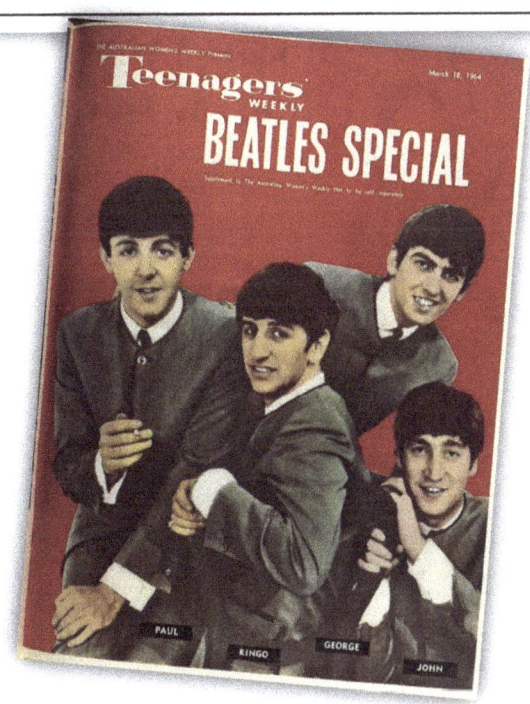

The LP and single that would launch the Beatles on the American market and start a musical earthquake: *I Want to Hold Your Hand / I Saw Her Standing There*.

ADVERTISING THE BEATLES

THE BEATLES
(Capitol-Swan-Vee Jay-BMI)
PM: Brian Epstein

NAMES: John Lennon, George Harrison, Paul McCartney, Ringo Starr. **AGES:** Early 20's. **HOME TOWN:** Liverpool, England. **BACKGROUND:** Rewrite an old adage to read: "There's no business like the record business." These four youngsters have created an international stir with "beatlemania," and have hit our shores with unprecedented impact. In less than a month their brand of music—the Liverpool (or Mersey) sound—has put them on the Hot 100 with three single disks, and one album, recreating a pattern established first in England. The irony is that they have been working together since 1958 in various cellar clubs in Liverpool. After an engagement in Germany, they were brought to the attention of their manager, Brian Epstein, who signed them with EMI's Parlophone label, and their success from that point on has continued to break records. They will personally visit the U. S. this month for television appearances on the Ed Sullivan show.

LATEST SINGLES: Positions on Billboard's Hot 100 this week are: "I Want to Hold Your Hand" (Capitol), No. 1; "She Loves You" (Swan), No. 21; "Please Please Me" (Vee Jay), No. 68. Bubbling in position 117 is the flip of their No. 1 record on Capitol, "I Saw Her Standing There."

LATEST ALBUM: "Meet the Beatles" (Capitol) is No. 92 on this weeks Top LP's.

Very quickly, almost every teenager in America was able to recite information about the four young men by heart.

ONLY **OFFICIAL** LICENSED NEMS ENT. LTD. '64.

BEATLE BOOSTER BUTTON IN COLOR

SIZE 3½" and 4"

AVAILABLE AT ONCE!

use for:
prizes
beatle parties
fan clubs
promotions
souvenirs

39¢ suggested Retail Price

100 per display box with card and window banner

weight 100 pins—7 lbs.

F.O.B. Chicago, Ill.
F.O.B. Philadelphia, Pa.

AREA DISTRIBUTORSHIPS NOW AVAILABLE

ACT NOW... Phone your Local Record Merchandiser or Distributor or contact the National Selling Agent...

Beatle Booster Button Company
care of Musical Isle Record Corp.
2429 W. Fond du Lac Ave.
Milwaukee 6, Wisconsin   Tel. 414—2644940 or 414—2644253

or

Beatle Booster Button Company
care of M.S. Distributing Co.
1700 So. Michigan
Chicago 16, Illinois   Tel. 312—3460865

The marketing world realized there was a ton of money to be made!

Even though Capitol Records had issued cease-and-desist orders, other labels were finding ways to cash in on Beatlemania.

BEATLEMANIA IS HERE!

England's #1 Recording Stars

have America's #1 Hit Single

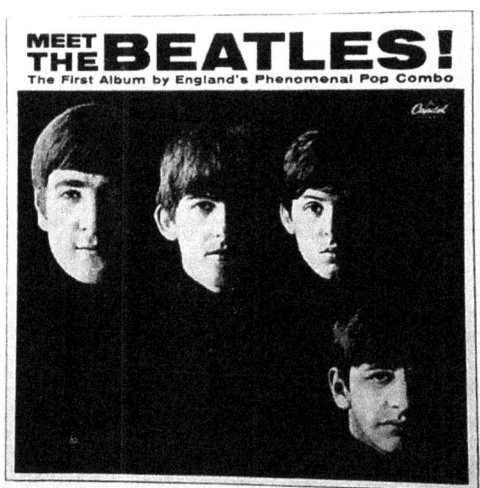

and America's #1 Hit Album

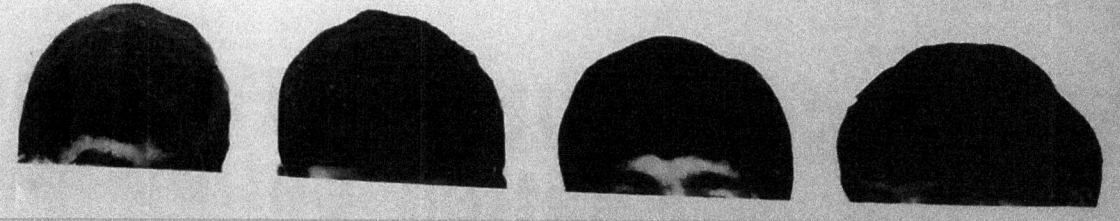

Ads began popping up everywhere for all types of Beatle-related merchandise.

The World's 4 best salesmen are coming back to sell Hohner Harmonicas!

Touring the United States from August 19th to September 20th.

This hotter-than-hot self mover from Hohner is going to hurry off your counter faster than tickets to a Beatle Concert! Kids have always loved harmonicas and now that the Beatles are blowing those sweet Hohner tunes, you're going to turn that love into a steady stream of EXTRA profits.

A "blister pack" combination designed for counter and rack display, each Beatle Package contains an especially designed 10-hole 20-reed harmonica that's similar to Hohner's world famed "Marine Band" model. This isn't a toy...it's a Hohner, which means that it's an outstanding musical instrument made by the best known company in the field. Also included are two of the Beatle's top song hits, a basic harmonica instruction chart and a signed photograph of that frantic foursome. The Beatles are making money for everybody. Put them to work for you!

Contact your wholesaler, or:

M. HOHNER, INC.
Andrews Road, Hicksville, L.I., N.Y.

Advertising the Beatles

The follow-up LP was out in the States within months of Meet the Beatles. Beatlemania was in full swing!

It's Here!
It's on Capitol!!
and It's ALL Beatles!!!

(S) T 2080

For the first time on any album their smash, number one single "She Loves You" and "Roll Over Beethoven." PLUS other great tunes ALL by the fantastic Beatles. Their first Capitol Album broke all sales records everywhere. And this one's going to break even THOSE records. THE Beatles albums are on Capitol.

And THE Beatles singles are too. "Can't Buy Me Love" b/w "You Can't Do That" (#5150) is an unprecedented hit, just released on Capitol. Within 2 weeks of release "Can't Buy Me Love" was #1 on the Billboard Chart — and your #1 money maker!

HAVE YOUR BUYER CALL CRDC AND ORDER IMMEDIATELY.

ADVERTISING THE BEATLES

Can't Buy Me Love was released in March 1964 with two million in advance sales, a record for advance sales at the time.

When you're only #7 in sales you must speak with straight tongue.

NINE HIT ALBUMS

MY FAVORITE SONGS FROM MARY POPPINS AND OTHER SONGS TO DELIGHT – RAY WALSTON AND HIS FAVORITE CHILDREN'S CHORUS   VJ-1110

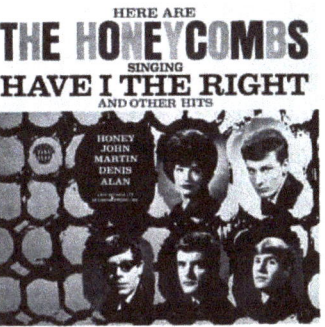

HERE ARE THE HONEYCOMBS   IN-88001

DELICIOUS TOGETHER – BETTY EVERETT & JERRY BUTLER   VJ-1099

BUBBLES – JOHN W. THAT IS   VJ-1109

LITTLE RICHARD IS BACK & THERE'S A WHOLE LOTTA SHAKIN' GOIN' ON   VJ-1107

THE BEATLES vs. THE FOUR SEASONS   DX-30

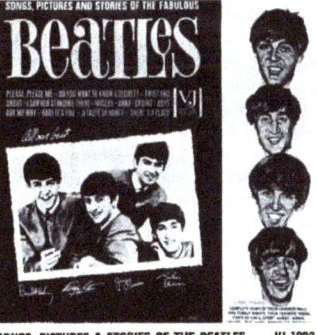

SONGS, PICTURES & STORIES OF THE BEATLES   VJ-1092

GOLDEN HITS OF THE FOUR SEASONS   VJ-1065

JIMMY REED AT SOUL CITY   VJ-1095

VEE-JAY RECORDS

ADVERTISING THE BEATLES

In the mad rush of Beatlemania, the other record labels that had initially enjoyed opportunities to release The Beatles' songs were still trying to cash in on the phenomenon. Capitol Records ultimately gained total control by October 1964.

The Beatles were everywhere, and Capitol was always eager to promote the latest appearance or release. This rare ad promotes a TV spot, a new EP release, plus Capitol's newest cash cow—an instrumental *Beatles Hits* LP.

For their first movie, *A Hard Day's Night*, the soundtrack was contracted to be released through United Artists, who were thrilled to get a piece of the Beatles' action.

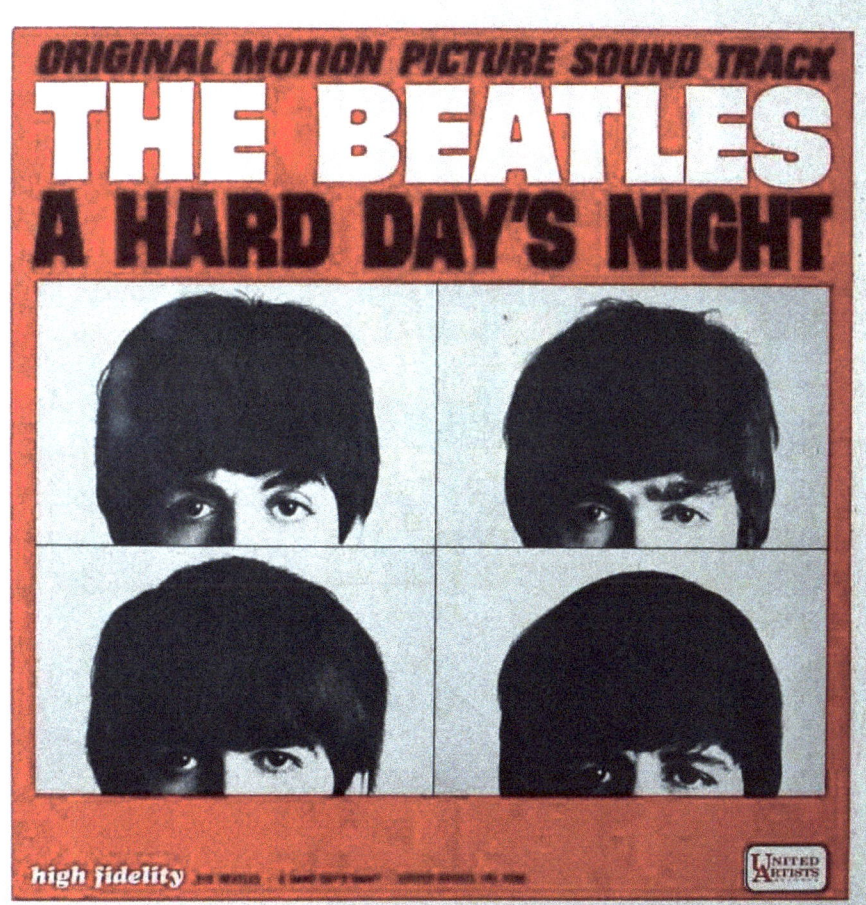

The flow of singles and LPs continued through 1964 at a rate never before seen in rock or recorded history. The ads above and opposite were for *Something New*, which included six new songs and previously released songs from *A Hard Day's Night*.

ADVERTISING THE BEATLES

Here come 6 new Beatles songs, plus 5 great hits from their first movie, all in one great new album:

(S)T 2108

Millions of Beatlemaniacs are waiting for *Something New*, right now! It's got 6 great new songs that aren't available on any other album, and it's got the best songs from the Beatles new movie, *A Hard Day's Night*, including "And I Love Her" and "I'll Cry Instead"!

("And I Love Her" #5235 and "I'll Cry Instead" #5234 are both on the charts right now, along with "A Hard Day's Night" #5222.)

So cash in on *Something New*, and take advantage of something new in Beatles prices. See your CRDC rep for Capitol's new one price to everybody: $2.02 mono, $2.53 stereo. (Album available beginning July 20.)

Then open the door, and stand back!

(Note: if you tear this ad out, and cut it along the dotted line, the top makes a great poster for your window. Let everybody know you've got the Beatles newest album!)

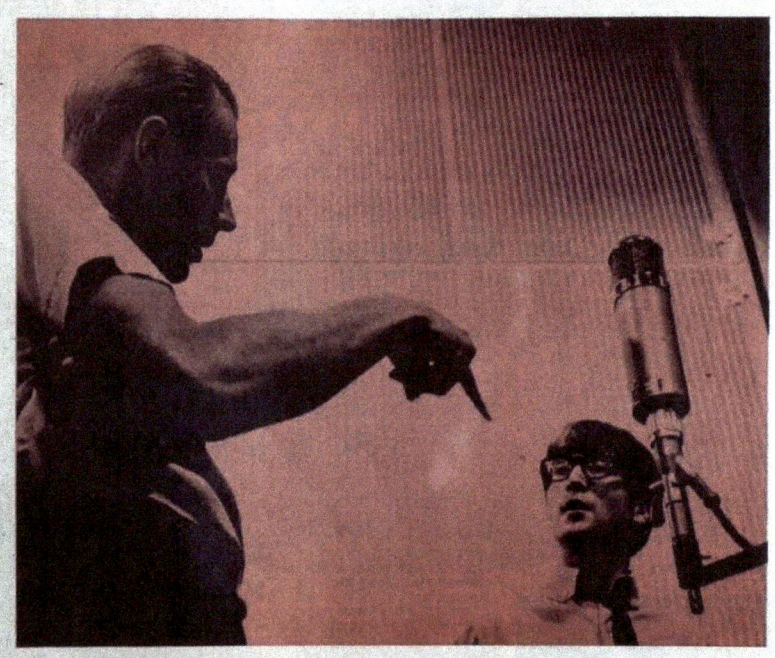

Even producer and Beatles' musical director George Martin got his productions into the trade magazines. This ad is for Martin's instrumentals, which were featured in The Beatles' movie.

ADVERTISING THE BEATLES

Perfect timing for profits! A smash new Beatles single combining two of the top hits from their smash album, "SOMETHING NEW!"

MATCHBOX b/w SLOW DOWN
(Ringo lead vocal)   (John Lennon vocal)

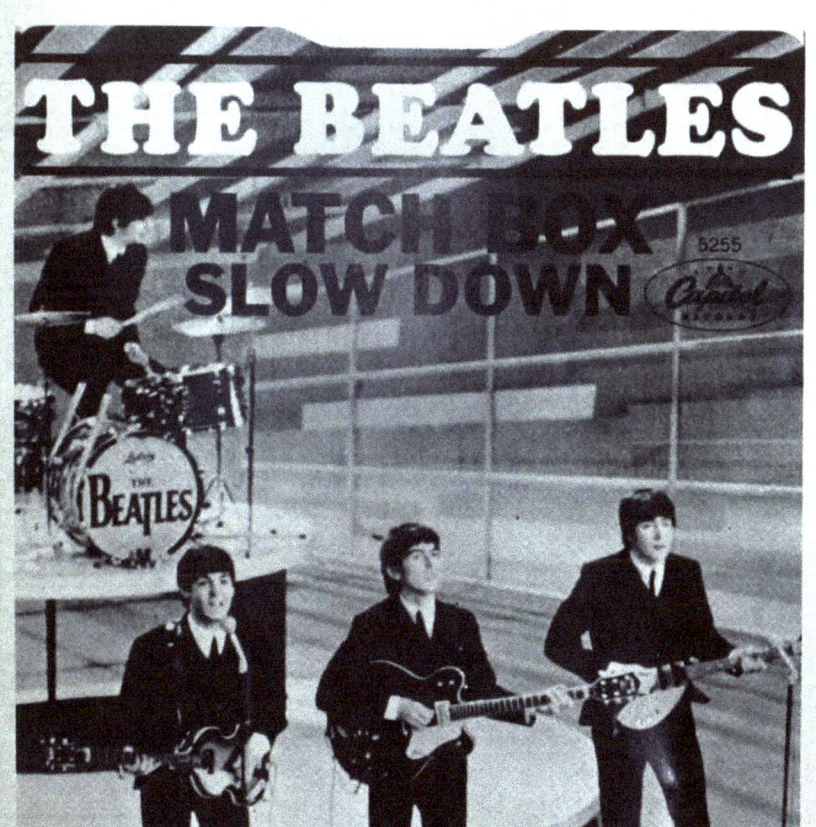
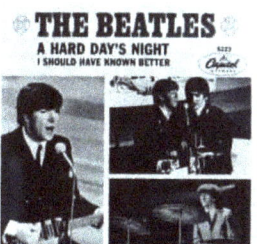
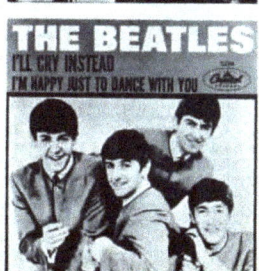
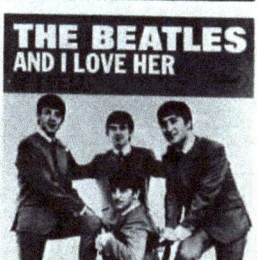

NEWEST OF FOUR CURRENT SINGLE HITS ON CAPITOL!

Advertising the Beatles

ADVERTISING THE BEATLES

This photo shows a typical record store window in 1964. Opposite are more ads for products. The Beatles rarely received compensation or royalties from the merchandising deals.

ADVERTISING THE BEATLES

A Capitol docu-record and a new single, plus ads for LP releases in Canada and one of the many parody songs released that were related to the band.

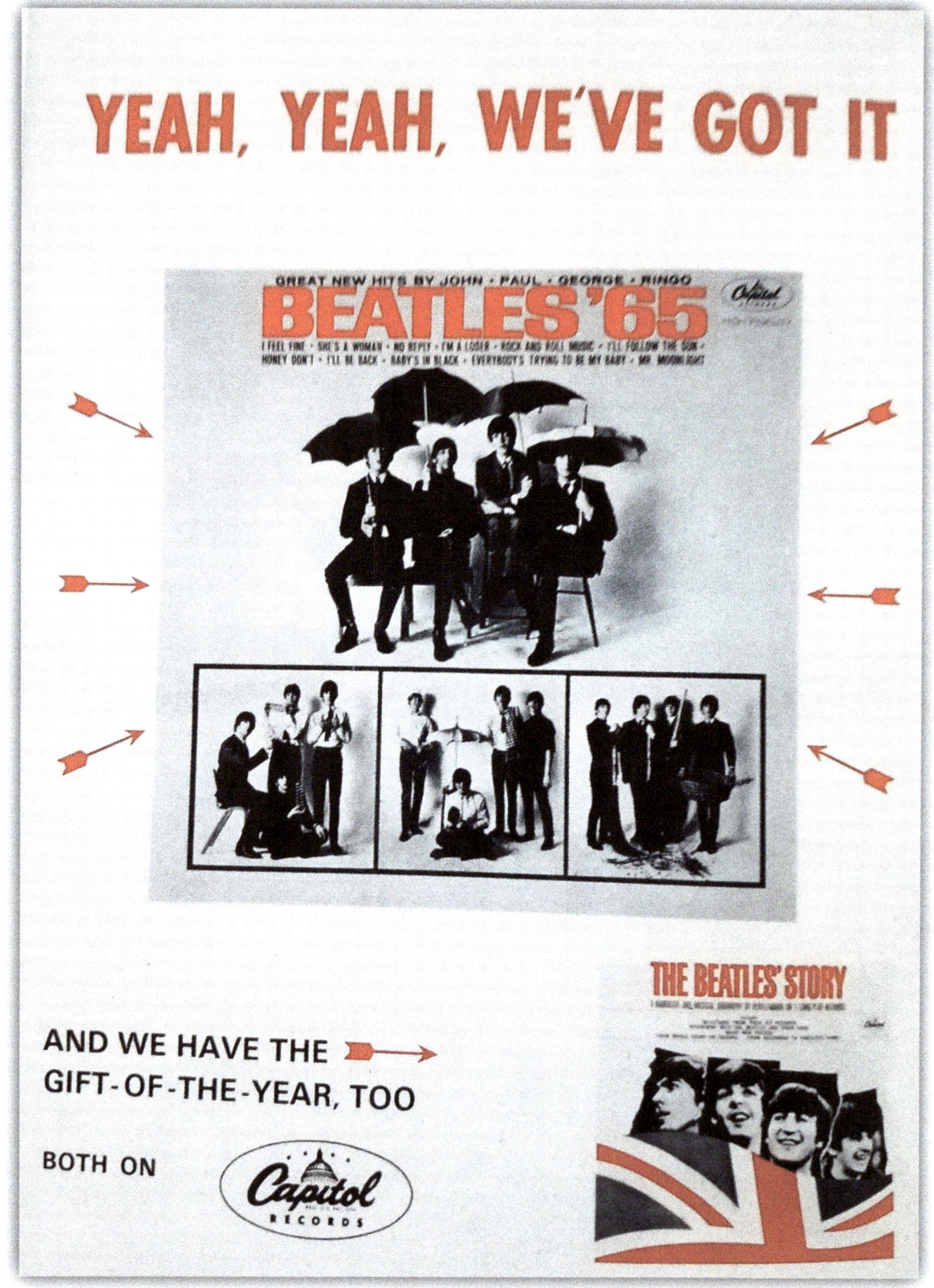

By the end of 1964, Capitol Records had released six LPs, seven singles and one EP. This was in addition to the numerous other titles released by assorted labels.

ADVERTISING THE BEATLES

More merchandise for the fans—who just couldn't get enough! The record player would go on to be one of the most desired pieces of memorabilia associated with the Beatles.

ADVERTISING THE BEATLES

The band started off 1965 with a new LP and another #1 single. There is also a rare ad for their amplifier company, VOX.

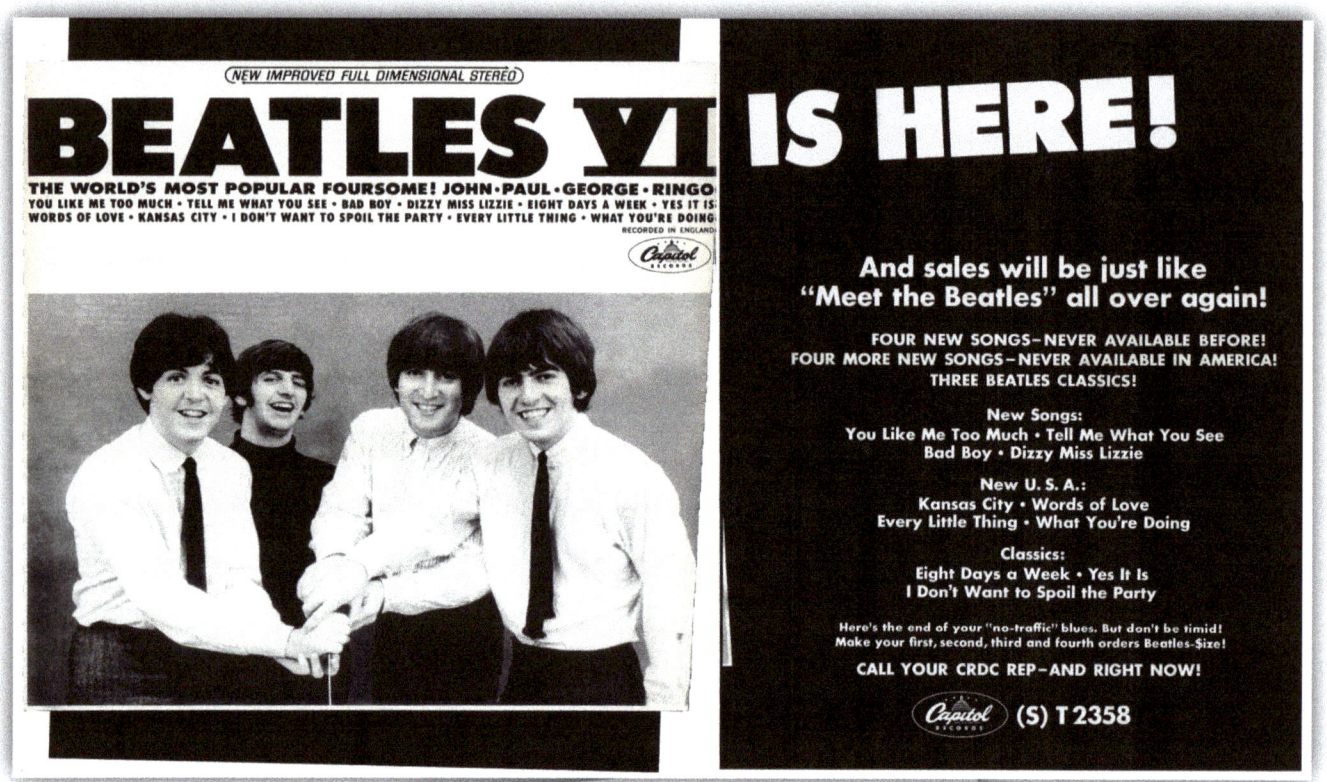

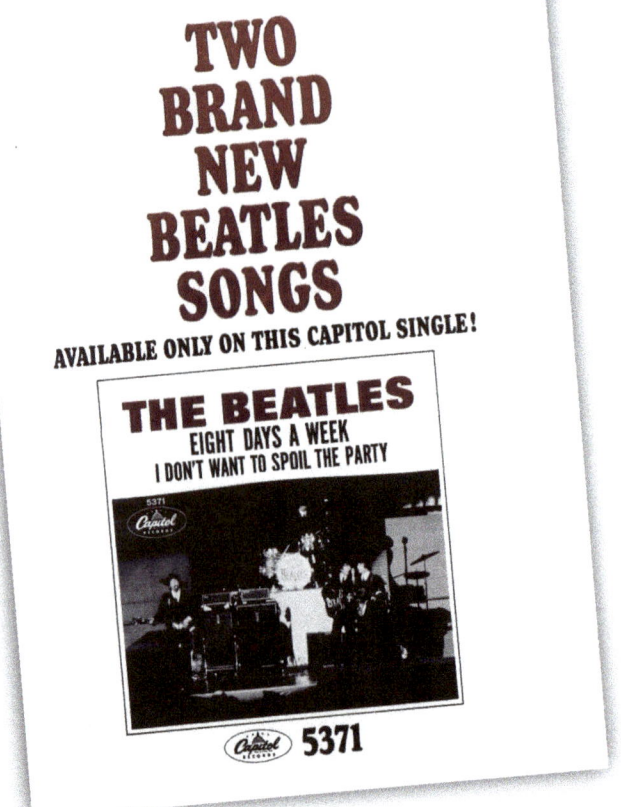

ADVERTISING THE BEATLES

Capitol prepared a colorful Christmas display that features the Beatles in Santa Claus outfits and has five tiered bins for holding the five Capitol Beatles albums available in December, 1964. The assembly instructions are shown above. The assembled display is over six feet tall. Its center panel shows the covers of the first four albums and states "happy holidays from the BEATLES."

Capitol's marketing department was in full swing with store promotions and record club ads.

ADVERTISING THE BEATLES

THANKS DJ's

"from us to you"

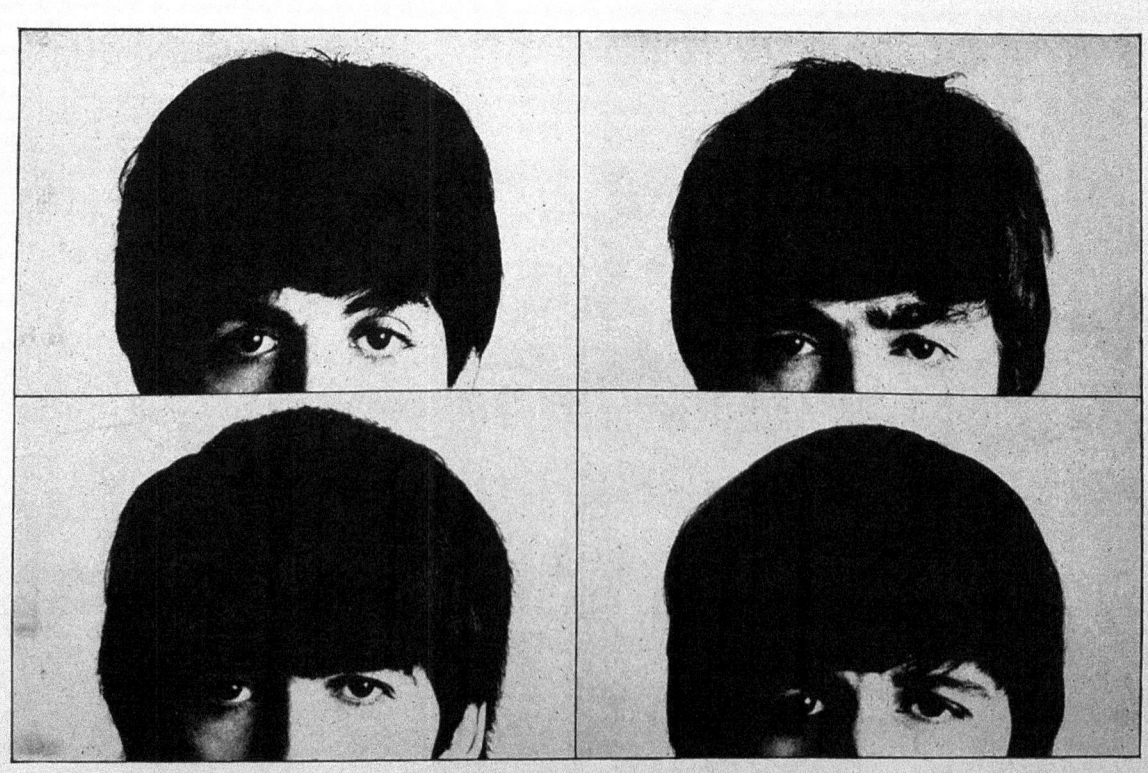

EMI Records Ltd.
London

NEMS Enterprises Ltd.
London

ANOTHER GREAT BEATLES 4-BY IN HARDBACK COVER!

1. Honey Don't 2. I'm a Loser b/w 1. Mr. Moonlight 2. Everybody's Trying to be My Baby

 **THE BEST OF "BEATLES '65"!** **R-5365**

Advertising the Beatles

A motorized HELP! display. This rare item opened up and the arms would rise, spelling out "HELP!"

ADVERTISING THE BEATLES

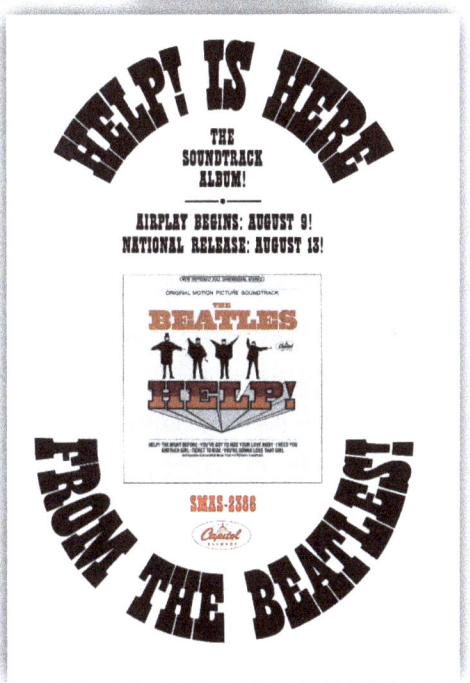

1965 saw the release of the Beatles' second film, *HELP!* and two new singles, *Ticket to Ride*, the *HELP!* single and LP release.

The height of Beatlemania was certainly reached at Shea Stadium in New York City. This was the largest concert ever held at that time. 1965 ended with Capitol still promoting *HELP!* and the newest landmark LP, *Rubber Soul*.

ADVERTISING THE BEATLES

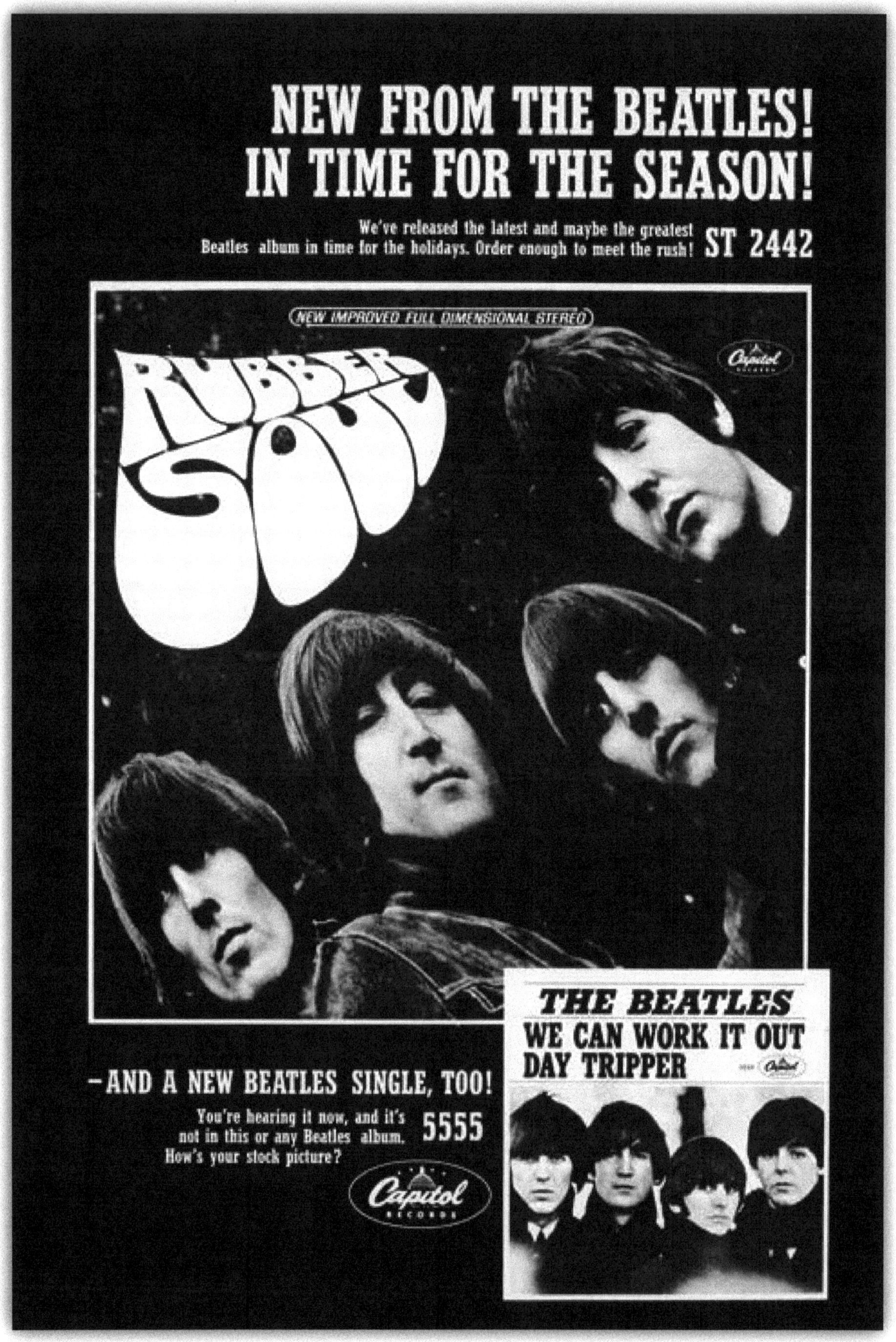

THE BEATLES
SING
12 BRAND NEW SONGS!
RUBBER SOUL
NEVER BEFORE AVAILABLE IN THE U.S.A.
GREAT FOR GIVING! OR JUST GROOVY LISTENING!
Capitol
NEW IMPROVED
RUBBER SOUL
Capitol

THE BEATLES
12 BRAND NEW SONGS
Never Before Available in the U.S.A.
Capitol
RUBBER SOUL
GREAT FOR GIVING!
OR JUST GROOVY LISTENING!

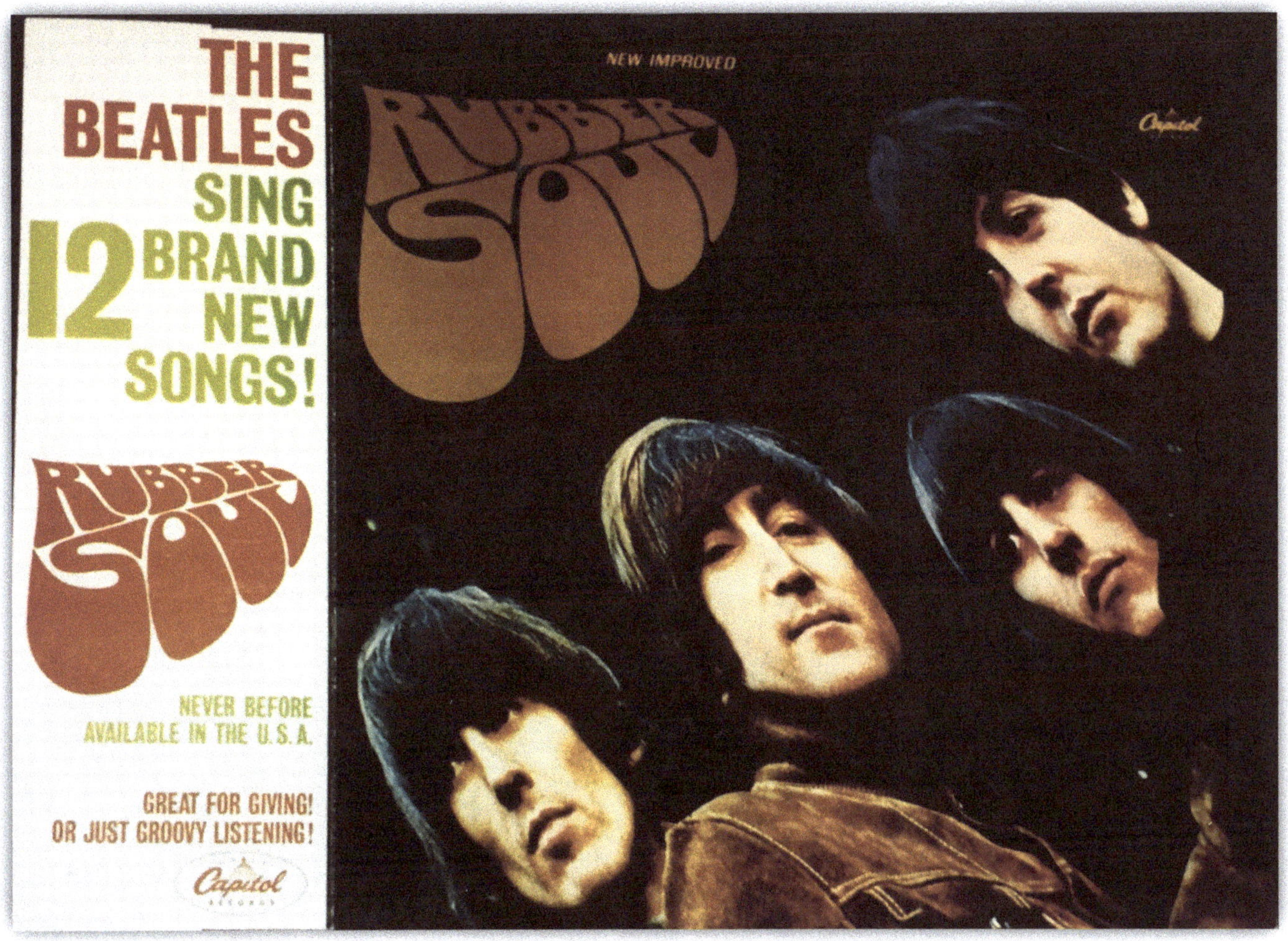

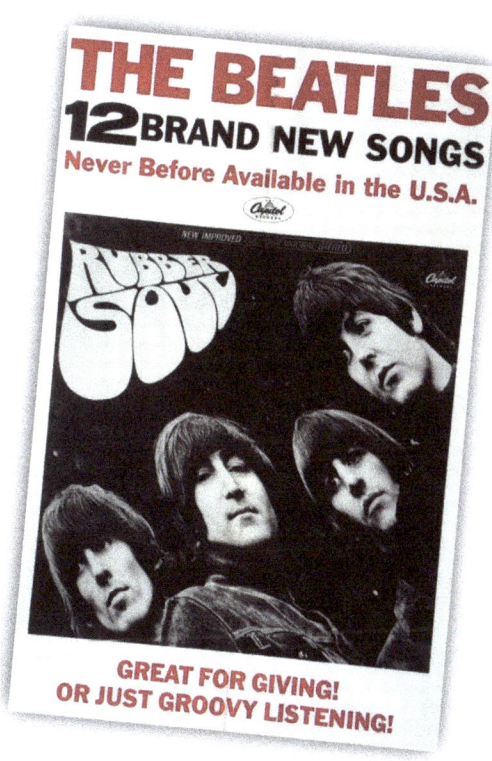

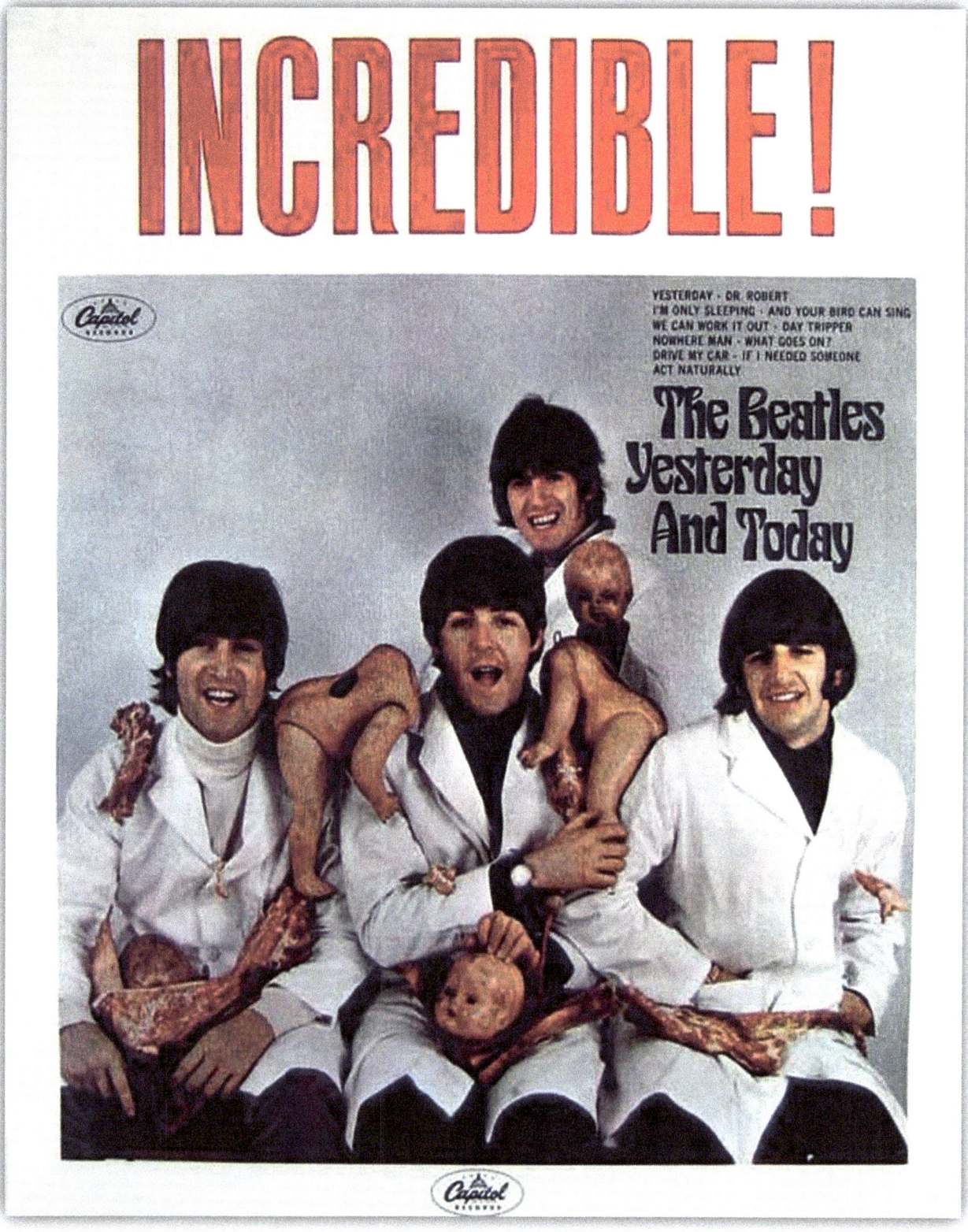

The release of the LP with its infamous "Butcher Cover" was a huge mistake that cost Capitol Records thousands of dollars. All the covers and promotional items needed to be scrapped.

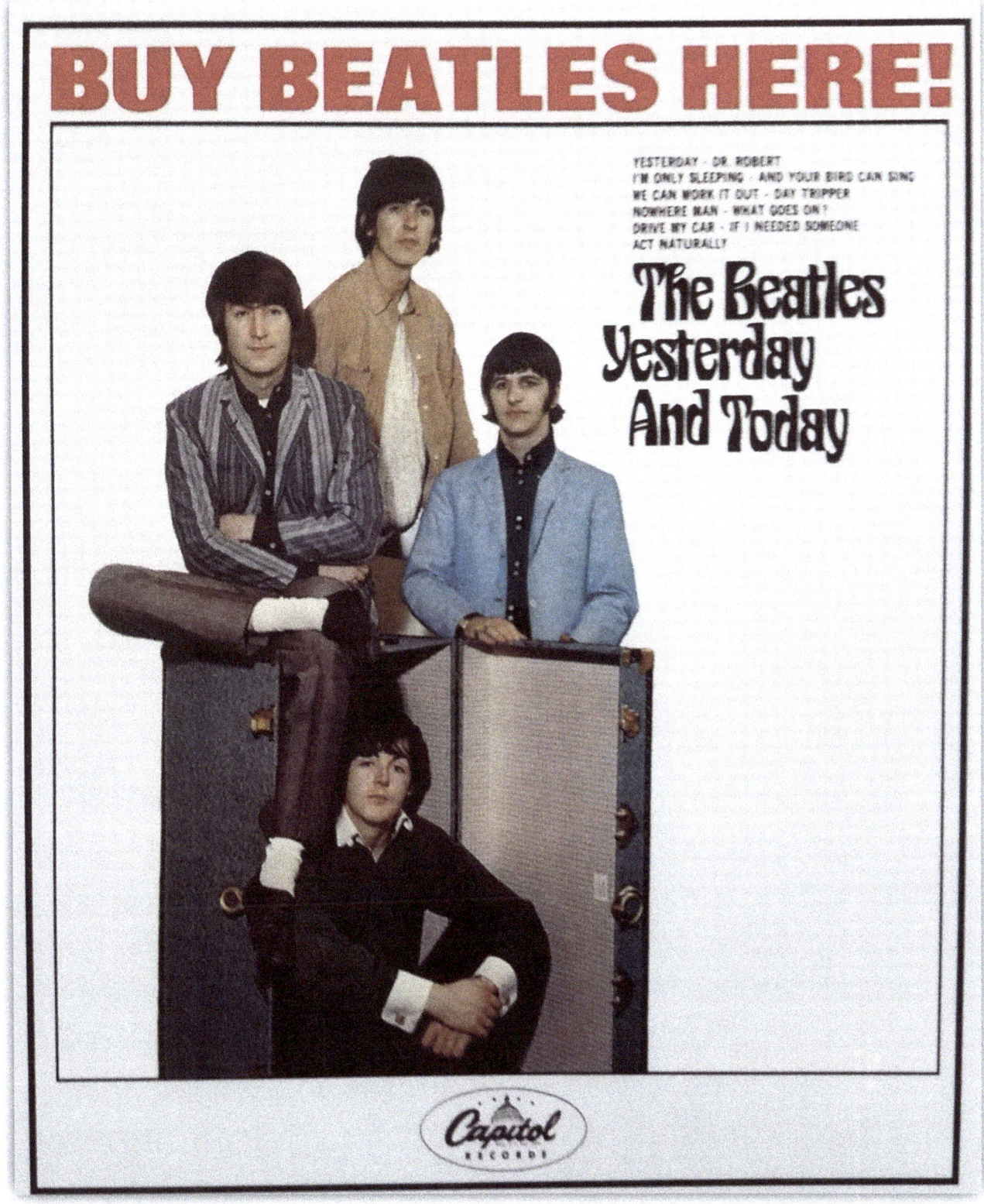

The new cover for the Yesterday and Today LP. Even to this day, collectors are peeling up the corners looking for the "other" cover; a few hundred thousand albums had the new cover glued on over the original.

ADVERTISING THE BEATLES

The ads on the following pages appeared throughout late 1965 and into the summer of 1966. You could even have your own Beatles headphones!

SELL
THE BEATLES
OWN LISTENING SYSTEM
beatLephones
Stereo headphones with full color photos of the Beatles on each earcup. And inside, a unique stereo sound that dramatizes stereo records as no other listening system can. Beatlephones offer personalized listening. Hefty sound for those who want to hear it; quiet for those who don't . . . even in the very same room. Beatlephones are the product of Koss Electronics Inc., makers of famous Koss Stereophones. So you can be sure of outstanding headphone quality.
It all adds up to fantastic sales potential among teen age record fans, guitar, accordion or organ musicians.
Order your trial quantity now or hear them at the NAMM Show. Booth 4 — North Hall. Conrad Hilton Hotel.
KOSS ELECTRONICS, INC.
2227 NORTH 31ST STREET • MILWAUKEE, WISCONSIN 53208
KOSS IMPETUS: 2 VIA BERNA • LUGANO, SWITZERLAND
* Manufactured under the exclusive license from FOMISA. $24.95 List
Write for complete catalog of products for the performer.

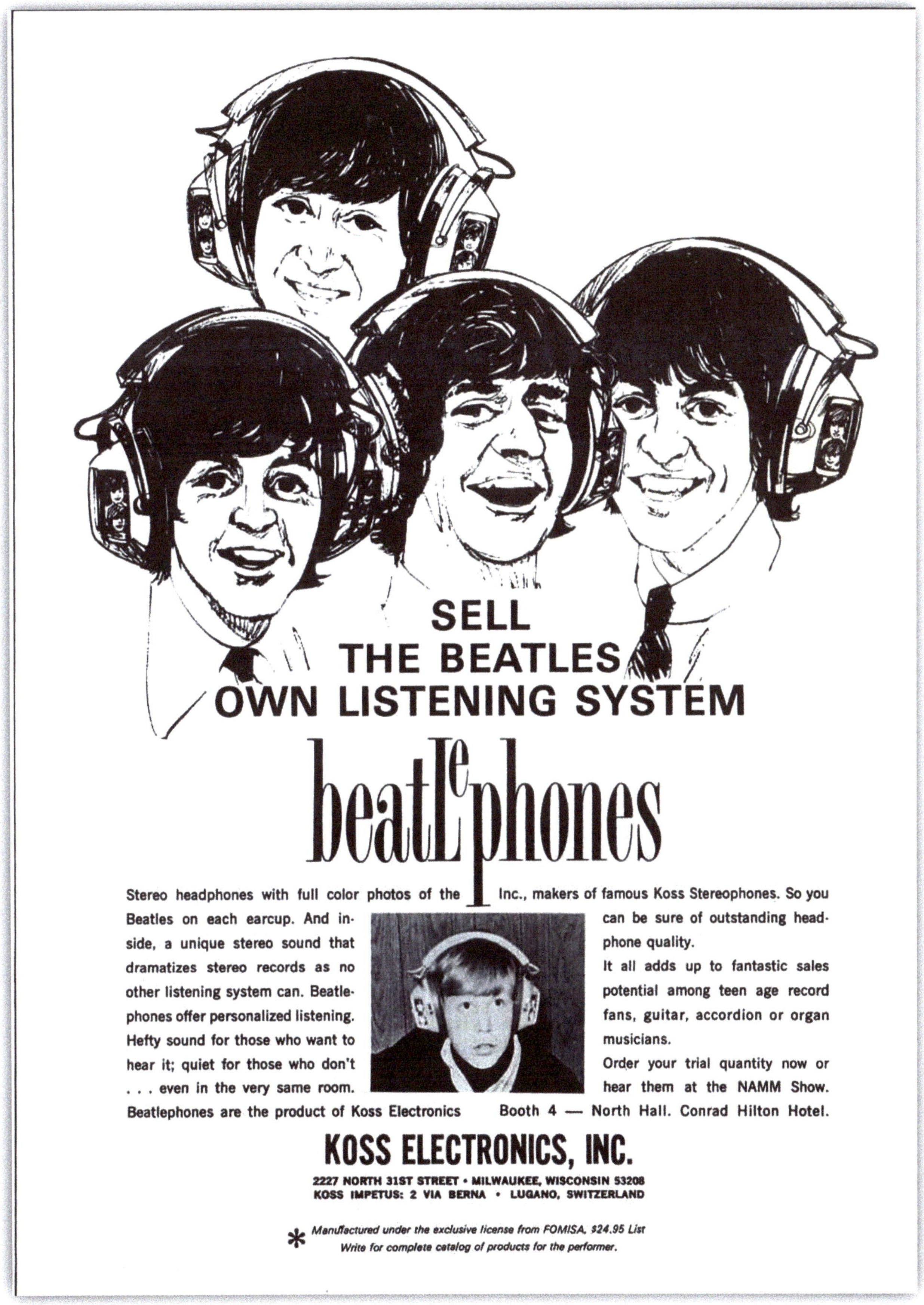

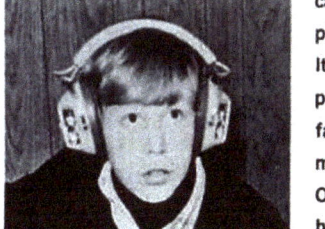

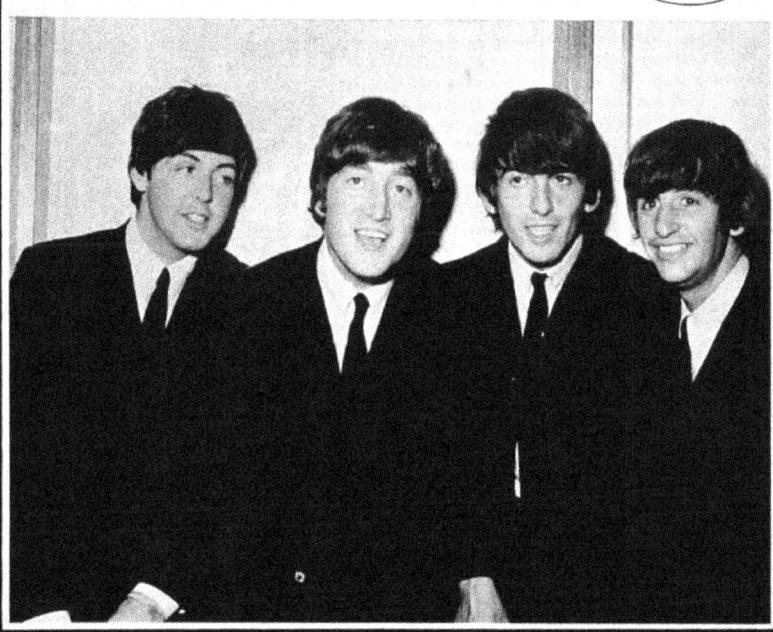

ADVERTISING THE BEATLES

ADVERTISING THE BEATLES

Revolver brought an end to what might be considered the Beatles' first era. Many believe that this record was the greatest rock LP ever. It opened up dozens of doors to future opportunities for the group in 1967 and beyond.

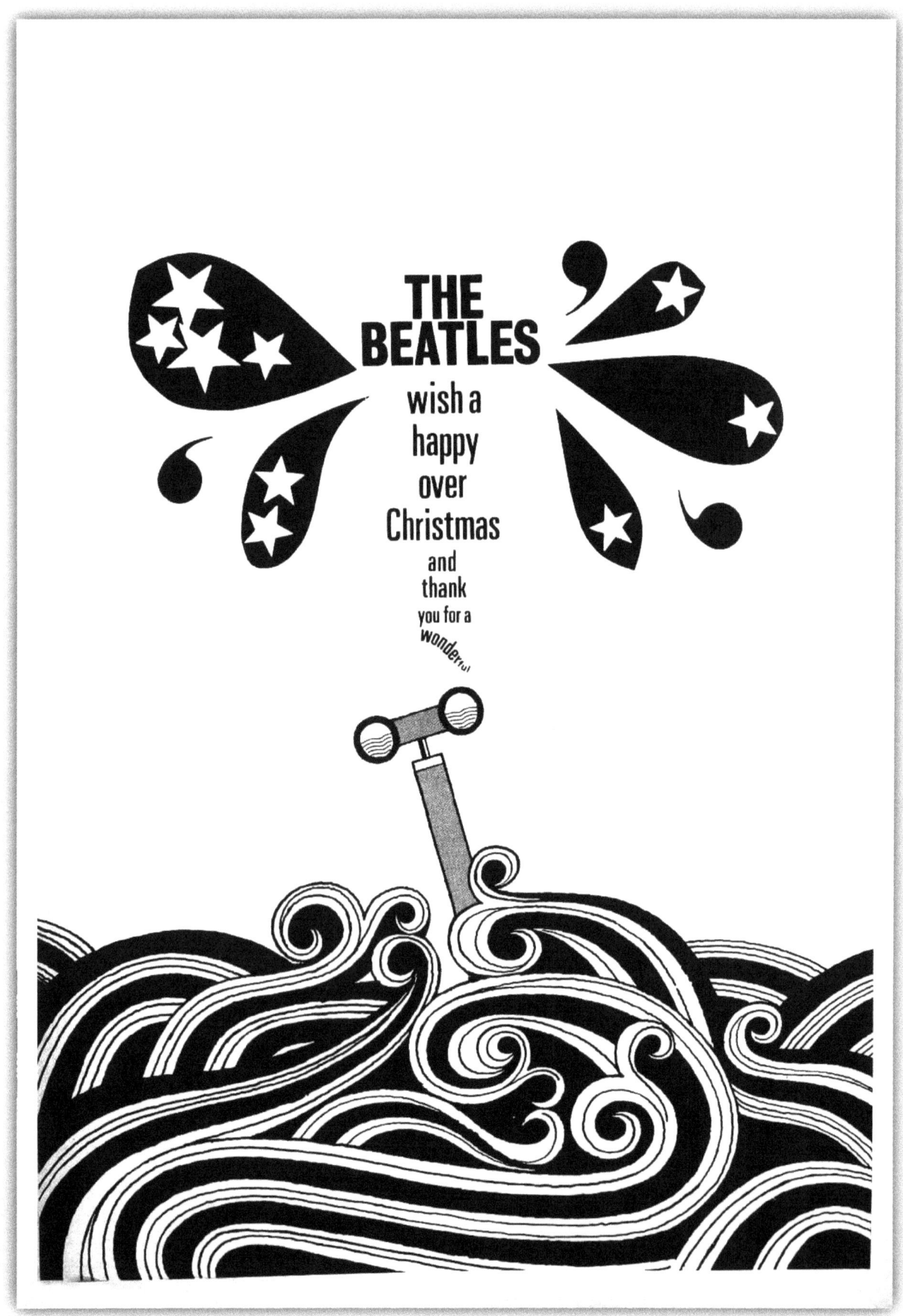

Advertising the Beatles

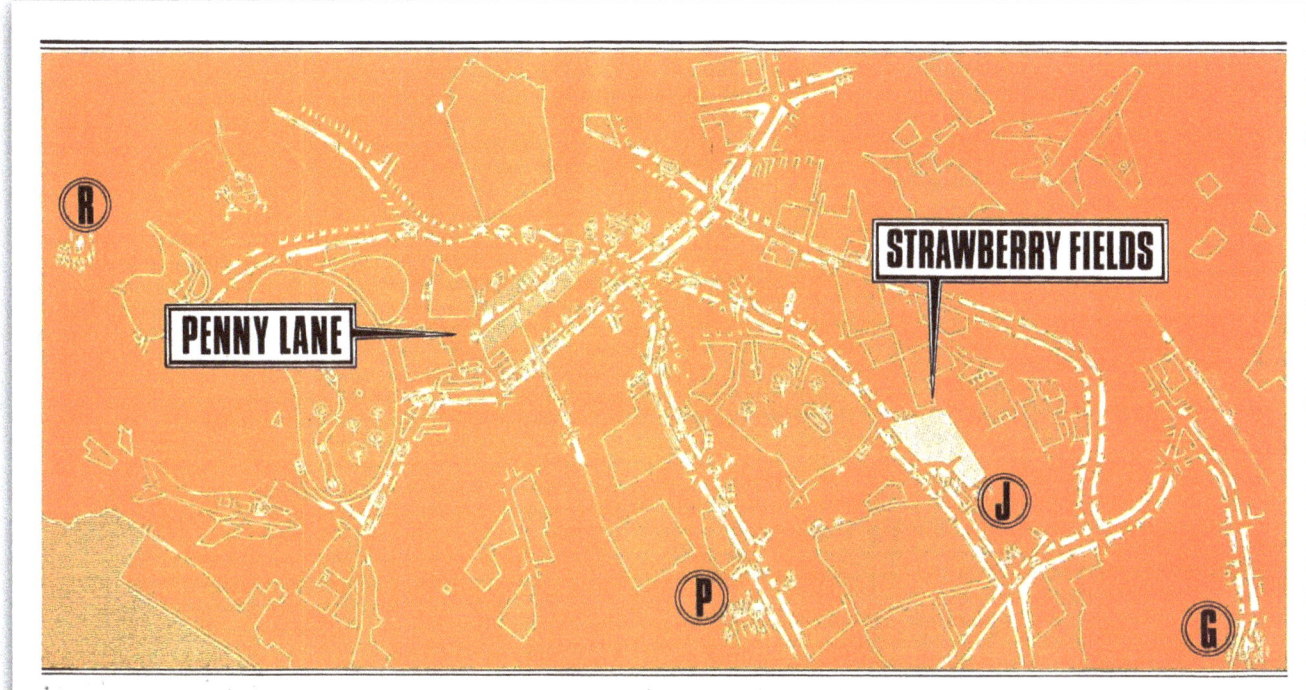

Sgt Pepper's Lonely Hearts Club Band—there will never be another one like it. This LP broke so many barriers and continued where *Revolver* left off. It was the sound of a new generation of music.

1967 brought the "Summer of Love." According to music experts and critics alike, iSgt Pepper, and following that, Magical Mystery Tour, would turn out to be two of their most influential albums: The band was as hot as ever.

Another anthem for that summer—released and recorded for a live TV special that was viewed around the world.

The last Capitol 45. All future releases would be on The Beatles' new Apple label. This switch sparked a new direction for their music; it appeared that psychedelia was over.

ADVERTISING THE BEATLES

the beatles
hey jude • revolution
apple records
2276

Hey Jude was Paul's homage to John's son, Julian. The ballad evolved from Hey Jules, a song widely accepted as being written to comfort Julian during his parents' divorce. Hey Jude would go on to be the biggest selling single in the band's career, not to mention one of the longest songs in the Beatles' catalog. The group debuted the new Apple Records label with this song,

1968 brought with it the band's most ambitious project to date: "The Beatles" —or as it would forever be known, *The White Album.*

Advertising the Beatles

ADVERTISING THE BEATLES

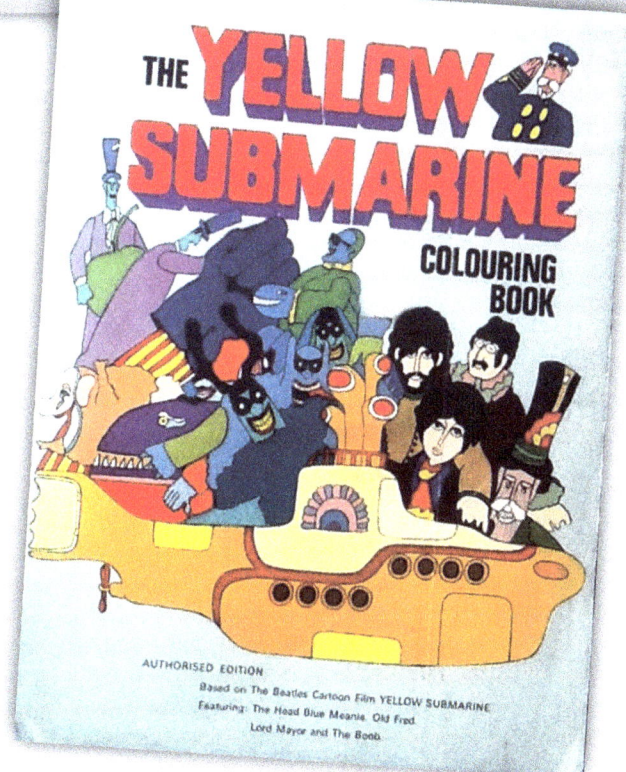

Next came the movie, *Yellow Submarine*, an animated film based on Ringo's 1966 song. Of course, it came with a soundtrack album and a merchandising campaign unheard of in rock before!

Advertising the Beatles

ADVERTISING THE BEATLES

Advertising the Beatles

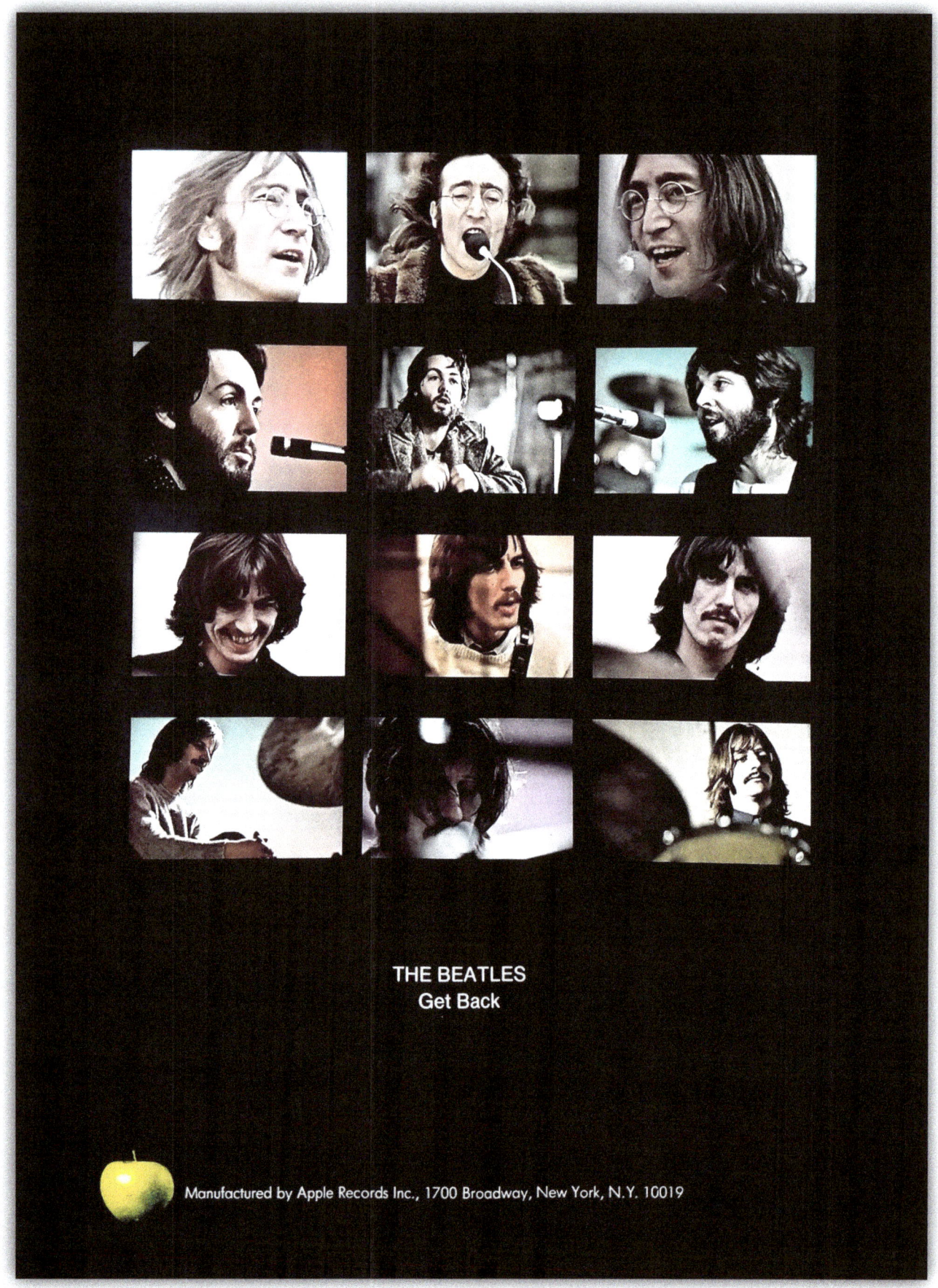

The Beatles as nature intended.

"Get Back" is the Beatles new single. It's the first Beatles record which is as live as can be, in this electronic age.

There's no electronic watchamacallit.

"Get Back" is a pure spring-time rock number.

On the other side there's an equally live number called "Don't let me down".

Paul's got this to say about Get Back... "we were sitting in the studio and we made it up out of thin air...we started to write words there and then...
when we finished it, we recorded it at Apple Studios and made it into a song to roller-coast by".

P.S. John adds, It's John playing the fab live guitar solo.

And now John on Don't let me down. John says don't let me down about "Don't let me down".

In "Get Back" and "Don't let me down", you'll find the Beatles, as nature intended.

Get Back / Don't let me down (Apple 2490)

Apple Records

ADVERTISING THE BEATLES

Early in 1969, we saw a quick release of a single that was recorded as part of a film project that would not see the light of day for almost another year.

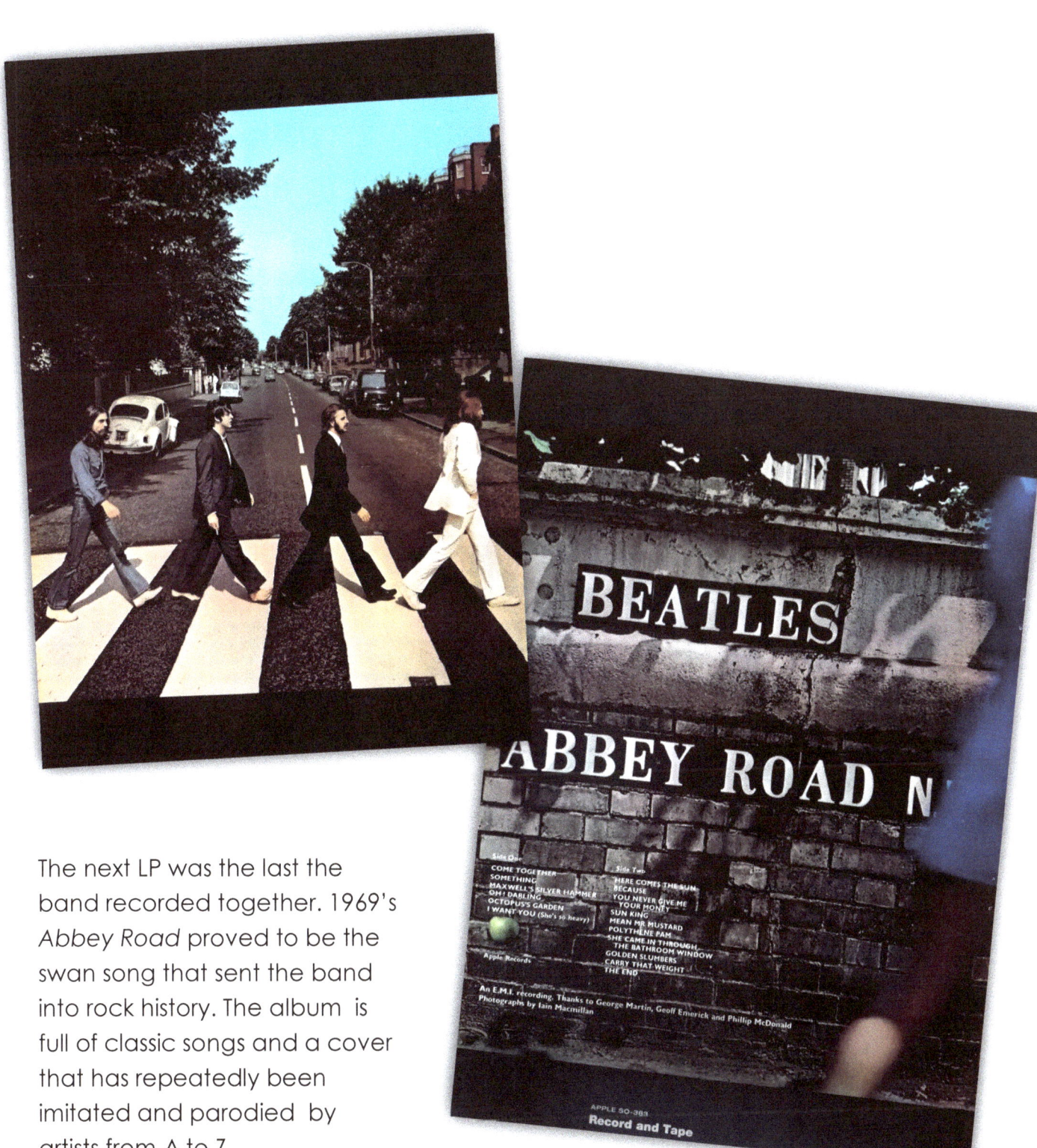

The next LP was the last the band recorded together. 1969's *Abbey Road* proved to be the swan song that sent the band into rock history. The album is full of classic songs and a cover that has repeatedly been imitated and parodied by artists from A to Z.

ADVERTISING THE BEATLES

ADVERTISING THE BEATLES

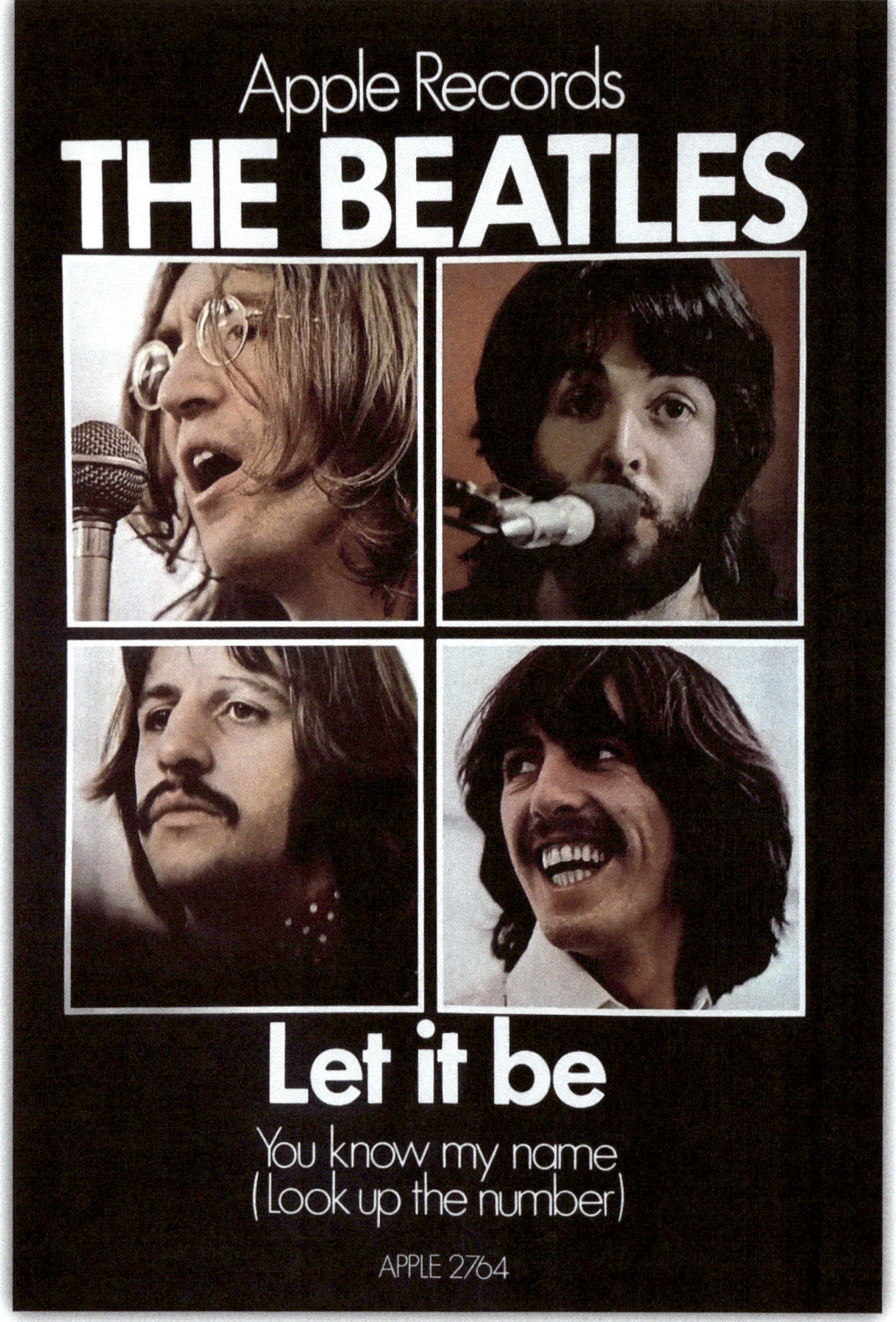

Recorded in 1969 and not released until 1970, the *Let It Be* film and soundtrack album showed the band at its rawest. Discord began to tear the group apart and many thought it would disband—until *Abbey Road* was released. The ads shown here are for the single release and the LP of the same name.

ADVERTISING THE BEATLES

Best Original Score Written For A Motion Picture
Or Television Special
LET IT BE
John Lennon, Paul McCartney, George Harrison, Ringo Starr

ADVERTISING THE BEATLES

One of the last British ads to run in the *New Musical Express* for *Let It Be* (1970).

LOOK WHO'S JOINED THE APPLE CLUB NOW!
END A MEAL WITH AN APPLE
IT'S NATURE'S TOOTHBRUSH

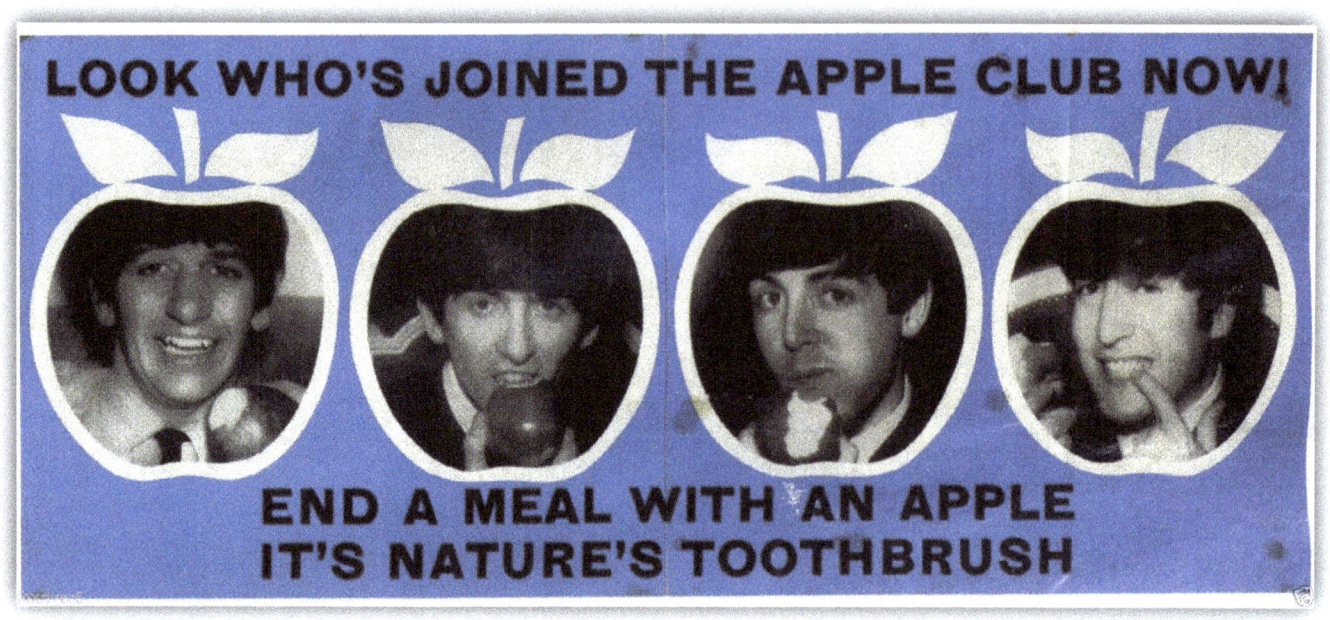

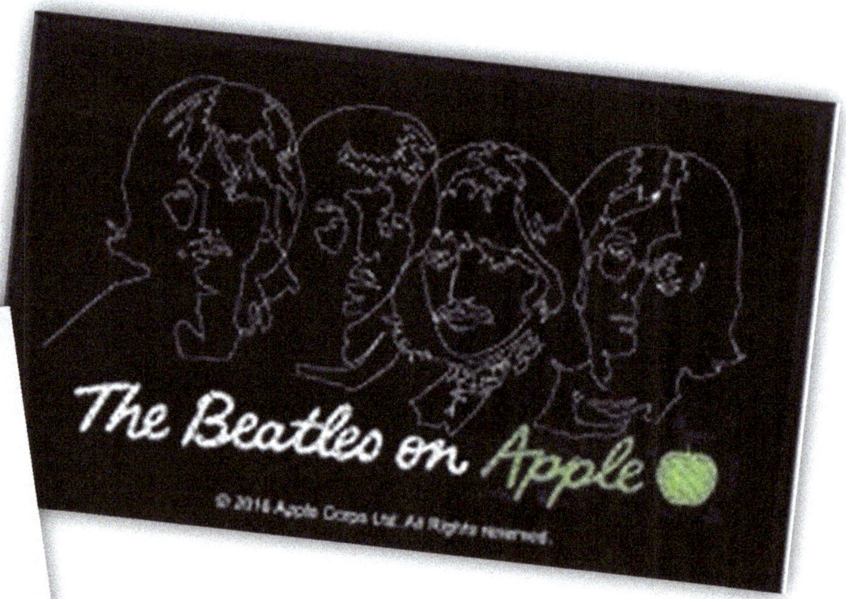
The Beatles on Apple

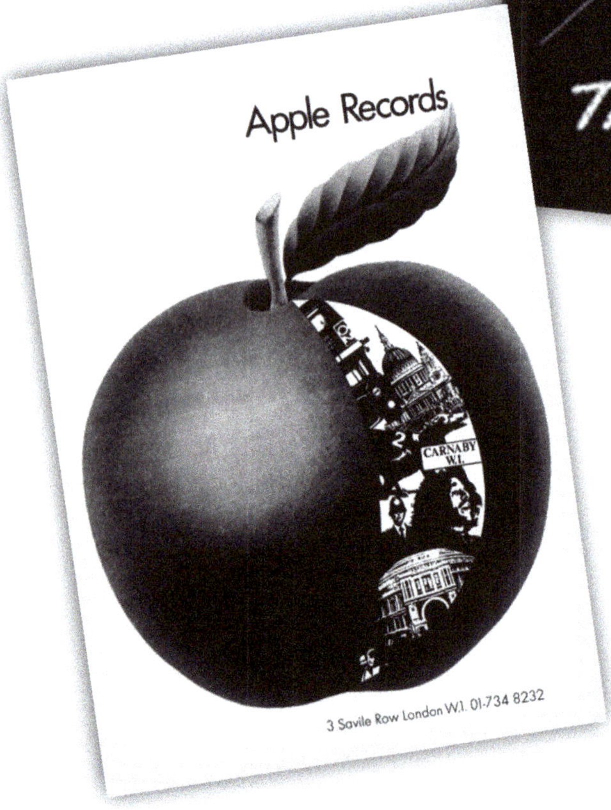
Apple Records
CARNABY W.1.
3 Savile Row London W.1. 01-734 8232

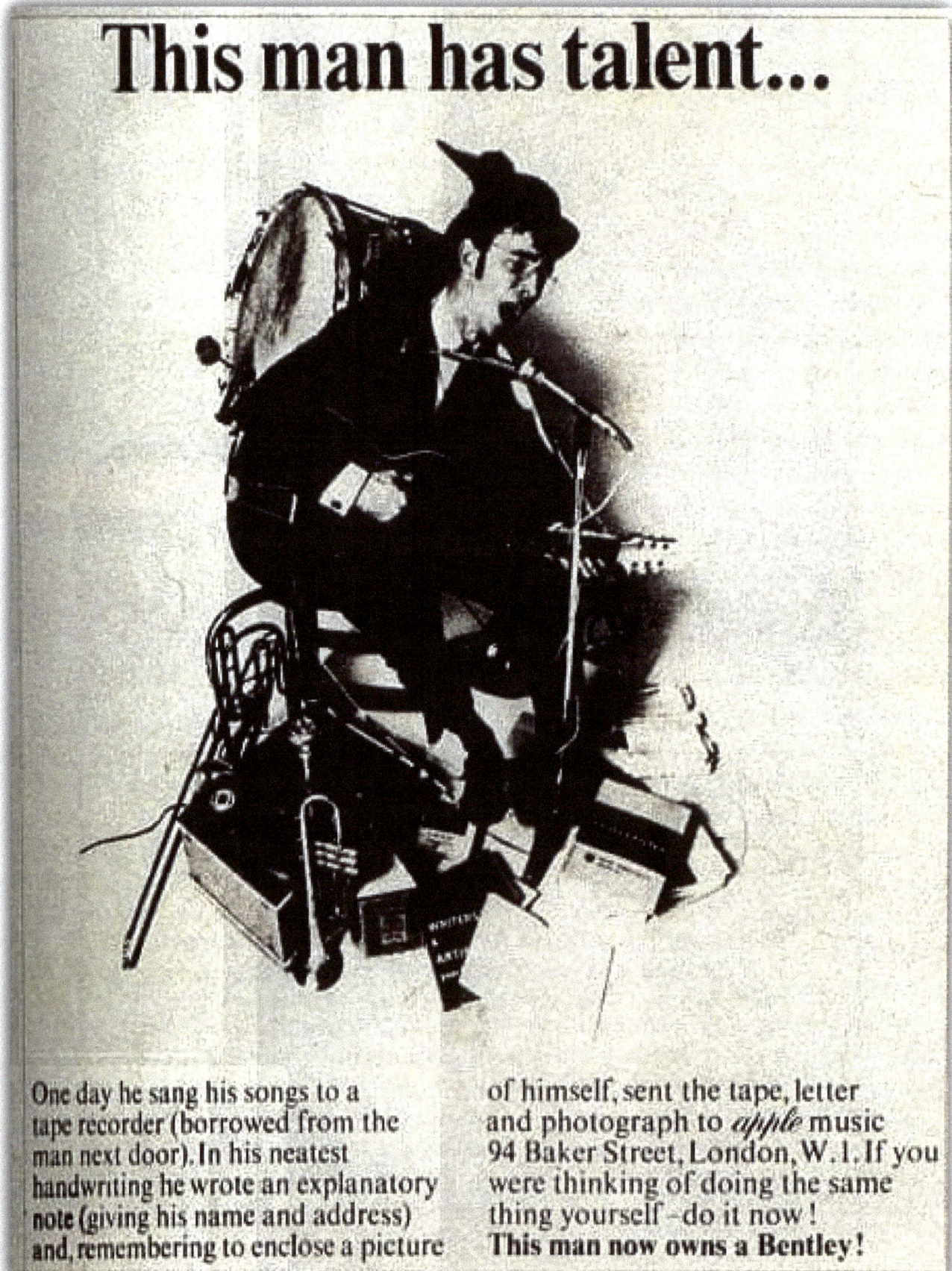

ACKNOWLEDGMENTS

Just a quick note to say thanks for all the help and encouragement I've received for this project.

First, a big thank you to my family for putting up with this obsession of mine. My wife, Marianne, has had to share me with these four guys since we met in 1979. Our kids, of course, were born into this, and now we have a grandson to whom I maybe can pass down some of the influence this band has had, and that will live on long after I'm gone.

Thanks also to all the Beatles folks I've had the pleasure and honor to meet along the way. On Facebook, I compare notes with a couple of different Beatles collectors. Thanks to Perry Cox and Bruce Spizer for their knowledge and their willingness to help a fellow Beatles nut with questions about memorabilia. Also to Erik McDonough and Pete Howard at Postercentral.com for the use of their images. Last but certainly not least, a thanks to life-long Beatles fan and great photographer, Wayne Beucher, for my author photo.

Thank you too to all the people who have had their Beatles books published and now fill my basement bookshelves.

Ray Zirkle

TWITTER:@AdvertisingThe1

E-MAIL:

www.rayzirklephotography@msn.com

BOOK FACEBOOK PAGE:

https://www.facebook.com/Beatleads/

www.ingramcontent.com/pod-product-compliance
Lightning Source LLC
Chambersburg PA
CBHW060940170426

43195CB00025B/2990